Is Muhammad in the Bible?

All Scripture quotations are from the King James Version of the Holy Bible.

Printed in the United States of America

ISBN 1-57558-123-X

Is Muhammad in the Bible?

Muslim Claims Examined in the Light of Scripture, History, and Current Events

Dr. Larry Spargimino

Dedicated to the countless number
of men and women who have given their lives
to share the Good News of Jesus Christ

". . . how beautiful are the feet of them that preach
the gospel of peace, and bring glad tidings of good things!"
(Rom. 10:15)

Table of Contents

Introduction

Since the publication of my first book on Islam, *Religion of Peace or Refuge for Terror?*, readers and listeners to our "Watchman on the Wall" programs of Southwest Radio Church Ministries have sent me volumes of materials relating to Islam. This is greatly appreciated. They have also informed me of an alarming increase in Muslim activities in their communities and neighborhoods.

In the fall of 2002, Muslim groups began targeting public libraries and community centers in America. Islamic speakers were given the opportunity to speak to the community about their religion which, they claimed, has been greatly maligned and misunderstood. These evangelists for the Muslim religion were given an opportunity to present Islam as being a religion of peace that has historically promoted women's liberation, human rights, freedom of expression, and liberty of conscience.

I have in my possession articles, tracts, brochures, and booklets that have been used to present Islam to the American public. On October 29, 2002, a Muslim apologist spoke at the Warr Acres (a suburb of Oklahoma City) Community Center and handed out literature published by the Institute of Islamic Information and Education. The titles of the tracts are as follows: *Human

Rights in Islam; Women's Liberation Through Islam; Muhammad in the Bible; Allah: The Creator and Lord of the Universe; What They Say About Muhammad; The Sword of Islam; The Question of Hijab; Moral System of Islam; Choosing Islam: One Man's Tale; and *Just One Message.* The material is slanted, historically inaccurate, and dangerously deceptive. I substantiate these charges in the following pages of this book.

I initially sought to write a ten-page booklet refuting the claim that Muhammad is mentioned several times in the Bible, and that he is the "Comforter" promised by Jesus in the New Testament. Noah W. Hutchings read the booklet, and also read the tracts published by the Institute of Islamic Information and Education. Upon doing so, he challenged me to expand my ten-page booklet into a book dealing with all of the issues mentioned in these tracts.

Richard Reid, the so-called "shoe bomber," managed to avoid detection by hiding his religious affiliations. He scavenged empty alcohol bottles (Muslims do not drink alcoholic beverages) and cigarette butts (nor do they smoke) from trash bins and left them in the hotel rooms where he had stayed. One researcher states: "To understand Richard Reid's behavior one needs to have grasped the basics of Islamic teaching: its maxim is that Islam should dominate the world. Whatever means are required to achieve this objective will be used, including deception."[1]

I have no controversy with Muslim people in general, whatever their ethnic background. We are *all* sinners who are unworthy of the grace and mercy of God. I do have a controversy, however, with Muslim apologists who insult the intelligence of the American public and treat us as though we are ignoramuses. Sadly to say, these apologists have been encouraged in this deception by the politically correct media and gullible government bureaucrats who love to tiptoe around controversial issues—all to the detriment of our great American Republic.

Chapter One

Is Muhammad in the Bible?

Is Muhammad in the Bible? In answer to this, many well-read Christians would retort, "How could he be? He was born in A.D. 570—several centuries after the canon of Scripture was closed."

For many Muslims, however, the answer to this question is: "Yes, Muhammad is mentioned several times in the Bible." In fact, the words of Deuteronomy 18:18–19—"I will raise them up a Prophet from among their brethren . . . And it shall come to pass, that whosoever will not hearken unto my words which he shall speak in my name, I will require it of him"—are understood by many Muslims as harsh words of warning to Christians for their refusal to follow the teachings of Muhammad. Why? Because, so they say, Muhammad is that "Prophet."

Muslims find support for the claim that Muhammad is in the Bible from the Koran, which states: "Those who follow the Apostle [Muhammad], the unlettered Prophet, whom they find mentioned in their own Scriptures, in the Torah and the Gospel . . ." (Surah 7:157). This is what the Koran says. But is it true?

"The Prophet Like Unto Moses"

The author of the tract *Muhammad in the Bible* asserts that "Muhammad is the prophet like unto Moses." He goes on to assert that the Ishmaelites qualify as "brethren" to the Jews and therefore Muhammad "perfectly fits" the description of Deuteronomy 18:15–18.

In Deuteronomy, however, the term "brethren" refers to fellow Israelites, not to foreign enemies. Muhammad and his people simply do not fit because they have never been friends to the Israelites.

A study of the relevant texts shows that "brethren" refers to members of the twelve tribes. In Deuteronomy 18:1–2 we read: "The priests the Levites, and all the tribe of Levi, shall have no part nor inheritance with Israel; they shall eat the offerings of the LORD made by fire, and his inheritance. Therefore shall they have no inheritance among their brethren. . . ." In this passage, the words "with Israel" and "their brethren" describe the same group. No room here for the Ishmaelites who are never categorized with "Israel."

Nehemiah 5:1 is emphatic: "And there was a great cry of the people and of their wives against **their brethren the Jews.**"

God's instructions to the Israelites regarding a king are also important. Deuteronomy 17:15 states: "Thou shalt in any wise set him king over thee, whom the LORD thy God shall choose: one from **among thy brethren** shalt thou set king over thee: thou mayest not set **a stranger** over thee, which is not thy brother."

There is no recorded instance when an individual from an enemy nation has ever been chosen to be king over Israel. That should not be surprising. While God promised that He would bless Ishmael, He nevertheless affirmed that His covenant would be through Isaac's line, not Ishmael's (Gen. 17:18–21; 21:12). The Prophet mentioned in Deuteronomy cannot be Muhammad. Far more consistent with the biblical and historical data is the New Testament's identification of who this Prophet really is. He is none other than Jesus Christ (see Acts 3:20–26).

We must also note that this Prophet of Deuteronomy 18 is like Moses (vss. 15,18). Significantly, there are many parallels between Moses and Jesus Christ. Like Moses, Jesus:

1. Was rescued from death as a baby (Matt. 2:13–23; Exod. 2:1–10);

2. Forsook the privileges of royalty (Phil. 2:5–8; Heb. 11:24–27);

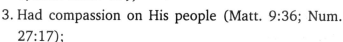

3. Had compassion on His people (Matt. 9:36; Num. 27:17);

4. Made intercession for the people (Heb. 7:25; Deut. 9:18); and was

5. Mediator of the covenant (Heb. 8:6–7; Deut. 29:1).

Muhammad simply does not fit. Unlike Jesus, Muhammad enjoyed many privileges of royalty, including dwelling in palaces, faring on sumptuous food, and having many wives. Muhammad was mediator of no covenant. Islam has no covenant.

7The assumption that the Ishmaelites qualify as "brethren" rests on the mistaken notion that the residents of the Arabian Peninsula are the children of Ishmael and therefore related to Abraham. Morey challenges this assumption:

> Abraham came from Shem while the Arabs came from Ham. Thus, it is no surprise to find that Arabia was already populated by the descendants of Ham, i.e., the Arabs, long before Abraham or Ishmael were born (Gen. 10:7). Their cities and temples have been well documented by archaeologists. At the time Ishmael was born, there were over a million Arabs in existence. This fact alone refutes the myth that Ishmael was the father of the Arabs.[2]

"Muhammad the Comforter"

In the above-cited tract, *Muhammad in the Bible,* we read: "It was Prophet Muhammad (peace be upon him) who was the Paraclete, the Comforter, helper, admonisher sent by God after Jesus. He testified of Jesus, taught new things which could not be borne at Jesus' time; he spoke what he heard (revelation); he dwells with believers (through his well-preserved teachings). . . ."

In their book *Unveiling Islam,* former Muslims Ergun and Emir Caner call Muhammad a "warrior prophet" and state that

> Muhammad himself gave the example for Jihad (fighting; holy war). . . . The greatest difference between Jesus Christ as God and Savior and Muhammad as prophet of Allah, comes at this point. Jesus Christ shed His own blood on the cross so that people could come to God. Muhammad shed other people's blood so that his constituents could have political power throughout the Arabian Peninsula.[3]

That anyone would equate the Prophet of Islam with the Comforter of the New Testament is a grievous insult. Yet we hear of no Christian organization issuing fatwas and death threats against Muslim leaders and organizations.

Contrast this with the bloody riots in Nigeria as angry Muslims rioted over the Miss World beauty pageant that was originally going to be hosted by Nigeria. According to a report in *The Guardian* (November 26, 2002) the riots have led to the death of two hundred people and the hospitalization of twelve hundred. In the aftermath, twelve thousand have been left homeless.

Muslim Apologists Wrest Scripture

While Muslims claim that the Bible has been corrupted and that only the Koran has the whole truth, it is interesting to note that Muslims will quote from the Bible when it suits their purposes and in order to make their point. So let's quote from the Bible to see if they have made their point, or missed it entirely. Is Muhammad really the Comforter?

In John 14 we read of the Paraclete, or Comforter. Even a cursory reading of the passage shows that Muhammad could not be this Comforter. Jesus said, "And I will pray the Father, and he will give **you** another Comforter" (vs. 16). The "you" is a reference to the disciples who were alive when Jesus spoke these words in A.D 33. Muhammad was born in A.D 570—several centuries later—far too late to fit the promise. If Muhammad is the Comforter, Jesus' promise never materialized and He failed His own disciples because they were left "comfortless."

Jesus also promised the disciples that the Comforter will "abide with you for ever" (vs. 16). Since Muhammad died in A.D. 632, he did not abide with anyone "forever." Again, Muhammad fails to meet the stated criteria of Jesus' own words.

Muslims try to squirm out of this "problem" by asserting that Muhammad lives forever with the disciples through his "well-preserved teachings." This again fails to meet the stated criteria of Jesus' words. Jesus was not promising "well-preserved teachings," but the presence of a Divine Person: "But the Comforter, **which is the Holy Ghost,** whom the Father will send in my name, **he** shall teach you all things" (vs. 26; see also John 16:13).

Whose "Stammering Lips"?

The author of the above-cited tract also finds Muhammad in Isaiah 28:11: "For with stammering lips and another tongue will he speak to this people." "This latter verse," states the writer, "correctly describes the 'stammering lips' of Prophet Muhammad reflecting the state of tension and concentration he went through at the time of revelation." While it is well-documented that Muhammad's religious experiences were accompanied by symptoms resembling epilepsy, it is doubtful if Isaiah's reference is to Muhammad.

A basic principle of interpreting Scripture, or any written document, is to let the context control the meaning of a phrase. There is absolutely nothing in the context of Isaiah 28 that even remotely suggests that Isaiah had Muhammad in mind. Isaiah 28:1 states: "Woe to the crown of pride, to the drunkards of Ephraim, whose glorious beauty is a fading flower, which are on the head of the fat valleys of them that are overcome with wine!"

Isaiah is giving a series of pronouncements against the northern kingdom, known for its most prominent tribe, Ephraim (vss. 1–13), and the southern kingdom, associated with the city of Jerusalem (vss. 14–29).

Isaiah warns his audience of the impending Assyrian invasion which brought the northern kingdom to ruin in A.D 721. The "stammering lips," therefore, are not the lips of the Prophet Muhammad in a religious trance, but rather the foreign languages of the invading Assyrians, which was "stammering" to the Hebrews. Significantly, the Hebrew word translated "stammering" literally means "foreign." Since the drunkards of Ephraim would not listen to Isaiah, God's response is that they would be enslaved by foreigners who would speak to them in a foreign tongue.

The Ishmaelites and the Kingdom

In another section of the tract *Muhammad in the Bible,* we read in the New Testament promises that there will be a shift of religious leadership from Israel to the descendants of Ishmael. The author states that "following the rejection of the last Israelite Prophet, Jesus, it was about time that God's promise to make Ishmael a great nation, be fulfilled (Gen. 21:13,18)." The tract argues that when Jesus stated: "The kingdom of God shall be taken from you, and given to a nation bringing forth the fruits thereof" (Matt. 21:43), He really meant "that nation of Ishmael's descendants."

I certainly don't want to deny that Ishmael's descendants have been richly blessed by God. At the present time, many in the Middle East possess great wealth in oil and a land area many times larger than that of Israel. Moreover, during the Middle Ages, when Europe was languishing in superstition and ignorance, Muslim centers of learning were putting forth scholars who excelled in science, astronomy, cartography, and architecture. The pointed arch, used in many European cathedrals, was developed in the Muslim world. However, it is doubtful if this is the subject matter of Matthew 21. What "nation" did Jesus mean when he said "the kingdom of God shall be . . . given to a nation bringing forth the fruits thereof"?

Since God has made unconditional covenant promises to Abraham concerning the nation and people of Israel, "nation" refers to Israel in the Millennium, that time when God's promises will be perfectly and completely fulfilled.

The Bible reveals that in the future God will pour forth His Spirit on the Jewish nation (Ezek. 36:26–28; Zech. 12:10; 13:1), which will produce "a nation bringing forth the fruits thereof." Israel will go through difficult times, but that is not a permanent condition. "Jerusalem shall be trodden down of the Gentiles, **until** the times of the Gentiles be fulfilled" (Luke 21:24; cf. Rom. 11:25). Christ wept over Jerusalem, and then made a promise: "For I say unto you, Ye shall not see me henceforth, **till ye shall say, Blessed is he that cometh in the name of the Lord**" (Matt. 23:39). Where do the Ishmaelites fit into this picture? They don't.

The Rejected Stone

In Matthew 21 Jesus tells the parable of the wicked husbandmen. In verse 42 we read: "Jesus saith unto them, Did ye never read in the scriptures, The stone which the builders rejected, the same is become the head of the corner: This is the Lord's doing, and it is marvellous in our eyes?" The author of the above-cited tract claims that the rejected "stone" of verse 42 is "that nation of Ishmael's descendants . . . which was victorious against all su-per-powers of its time as prophesied by Jesus."

That interpretation is founded on nothing more sub-stantial than wishful thinking. "The stone" is not a na-tion—"that nation of Ishmael's descendants," or any oth-er nation for that matter—but a Person, the Lord Jesus Christ.

In the parable of the wicked husbandmen, no nation is mentioned. The husbandmen reject "the son" (Matt. 21:38–40). In this parable, the householder represents God, and the abused servants sent by the householder represent the Hebrew prophets who had been mistreated and abused by the Jewish religious leaders. The words, "but last of all he sent unto them his son," indicate that Jesus was God's final messenger to Israel.

Our Lord is telling His audience how He will be treat-ed by His own people. Jesus was rejected as prophesied (Isa. 53:3), but His rejection is not final. "The stone which the builders rejected [Jesus Christ], the same is become the head of the corner" (Matt. 21:42). First Peter 2:6 con-firms this interpretation that the "stone" is Jesus Christ. "Wherefore also it is contained in the scripture, Behold, I lay in Sion a chief corner stone, elect, precious: and he that believeth **on him** shall not be confounded."

Are Mecca and Medina Mentioned in Scripture?

Muslims find Muslim shrines, sites, and religious loca-tions mentioned in the Bible. For example in the tract *Muhammad in the Bible* we read: "One of the signs of the prophet to come from Paran (Mecca) is that he will come with 'ten thousands of saints' (Deuteronomy 33:2 KJV). That is the number of faithful who accompanied Prophet

Muhammad to Paran (Mecca) in his victorious, bloodless return to his birth-place to destroy the remaining symbols of idolatry in the Ka'bah."

The author has conveniently forgotten to mention that it is not the Prophet Muhammad, or any human being, who comes from Paran. Deuteronomy 33:2 reads: "And he said, The LORD came from Sinai, and rose up from Seir unto them; he shined forth from mount Paran, and he came with ten thousands of saints: from his right hand went a fiery law for them."

In another passage in this same tract, the reader is told that "Habakkuk 3:3 speaks of God (God's help) coming from Te'man (an oasis north of Medina according to J. Hasting's Dictionary of the Bible), and the holy one (coming) from Paran. That holy one who under persecution migrated from Paran (Mecca) to be received enthusiastically in Medina was none but Prophet Muhammad."

In these passages "Mecca" is conveniently substituted for "Paran" and "Teman" is said to be "an oasis north of Medina according to J. Hasting's Dictionary of the Bible."

I don't have Hasting's Dictionary, so I can't check out the reference, but I do have several other Bible dictionaries and not a one makes any connection between Teman and Medina.

Ezekiel 25:13 speaks of judgment upon Edom (the area around Petra in modern Jordan) and says judgment on Edom will begin with Teman. This means that Teman is in the area of Petra, not Medina in Saudi Arabia.

Muslims try to find Muhammad in the Bible and they change place names to suit this agenda. Such a procedure is illegitimate. No credence should be given to any groups who change Scripture to make it say what they think it should. When Muslims try to build a case on place names, they commit a logical fallacy and a geographical one. Morey explains:

Muslim apologists such as Deedat, Badawi, and Shabir have assumed that if they can find in the Bible a passing reference to some place in Arabia, then this would automatically prove that Muhammad was in the Bible. Of course this is logically absurd!

Since the Bible refers to many ancient cities and countries, even if there were a reference to Mecca or Arabia, this would not logically prove anything. Do the biblical references to Babylon prove that the coming prophet would be a Babylonian? Of course not! . . . In addition to being based on a logical fallacy, the geographical arguments are not factual. The words that are used to link the Bible to Mecca or to Arabia are erroneous. The Bible refers to a place called "Baca" in Psalm 84:4–6. How do Muslims go from Baca to Mecca? They chant, "Baca, Maca, Mecca." They replace the "B" with an "M" and the "a" with an "e" and move from Baca to Mecca.

There are several problems with this argument. First, there is no logical justification for arbitrarily switching Hebrew letters. Second, there is no Hebrew manuscript that changes the spelling. Third, simply chanting a phonic fallacy cannot change the manuscript evidence. Fourth, in Psalm 84, Baca was a valley in northern Israel that was on the pilgrim pathway to Mt. Zion, a symbol for worship at the temple in Jerusalem.[4]

Chapter Two

Muhammad and His Followers on the Death and Resurrection of Christ

According to the Koran, Jesus only appeared to be crucified. Surah 4:157 states: "That they said in boast, 'we killed Christ Isa, the son of Mary' . . . but they killed him not, nor crucified him." Some Muslims claim that Judas Iscariot was crucified in his place, or someone else, but Jesus was not crucified.

This means that Muslims do not believe that Jesus Christ was resurrected from the dead. The reason? They do not believe that He was crucified. Someone else was crucified in His place. You cannot have a resurrection when there is no death. That's the reason for the apostle's statement in 1 Corinthians 15:3–4: "For I delivered unto you first of all that which I also received, how that *Christ died for our sins* . . . And that he was buried, and that he rose again the third day according to the scriptures."

The resurrection of Christ is a central tenet of the Christian faith. It rests on several lines of evidence.

1. Thousands of ancient manuscripts of the New Testament, early sermons, and quotations by early Christians tell of the resurrection of Christ.
2. Jesus was buried in a public tomb of a wealthy person, Joseph of Arimathea. There was nothing secretive or clandestine about the death and burial of Jesus.
3. Christ's death on the cross was a severe disappointment to His followers. They were, therefore, disposed *against* believing the resurrection. They needed something to happen that was of undeniable evidence for them to change their minds from fear to faith.
4. The tomb was empty and none of the ancient enemies of Christianity—Roman or Jewish—ever produced the body of Christ.
5. At different times, and under different circumstances, the disciples had experiences which they believed involved literal appearances of the risen Christ.
6. Many of the apostles and the early Christians, suffered martyr's deaths for their conviction that the resurrection had actually occurred.
7. The message that Jesus is alive is the central message of the Christian faith. If the enemies of Christianity wanted the most effective way of destroying Christianity, it would have been to produce the body of Jesus, but no one ever did.
8. Skeptics, doubters, and the fearful—such as Thomas, Paul, and Peter—became convinced of the resurrection of Jesus Christ. Something completely convincing must have occurred.

The Impact of the Resurrection

> Who shall change our vile body, that it may be fashioned like unto his glorious body, according to the working whereby he is able even to subdue all things unto himself.
> —Phil. 3:21

The early Christians were Jews. Those Christians who came from Gentile backgrounds, such as Cornelius, were very knowledgeable in Old Testament practices. However, the impact of the resurrection was so far-reaching that not only did it give them boldness in the face of death, but it gave them convincing warrant to abandon, or at least radically alter, many of their beliefs.

For one thing, the early Christians discarded the belief that animal sacrifices were a part of making atonement for one's sins. The significance of this is that these early Jewish Christians were so convinced that Jesus Christ was the Son of God that they were willing to abandon a practice that was at the very center of their faith. A dead Messiah would not have convinced anyone to change anything.

Secondly, they discarded the practice of following the Mosaic legislation, including the Sabbath, violations of which received the severest of judgments from God under the Old Covenant. Would a Jesus who promised to be raised by the power of God the third day—but actually was not—have provided them with the motivation to violate, or at least alter, these Old Testament requirements?

Moreover, these Jewish Christians abandoned hope in a political deliverer who, in their day, would destroy the Roman oppressors. They were willing, instead, to be oppressed because they believed in the infinite efficacy of the atoning sacrifice of the Son of God who died on the cross like a criminal. Ankerberg and Weldon write:

> Just look at the facts surrounding the earliest church.
> A crucified Jew, a despised tax collector, a hater of

Jesus who killed Christians, and a few fishermen began a movement that became the largest, most influential religion on earth—an impossibility unless the
resurrection really happened. Here is an obscure, un-
organized movement; struggling within the loins of
the ancient Roman Empire; arising within a conquered
people; subject to much opposition, persecution, and
suppression from the religious authorities; based entirely upon a single controversial Jew whose followers
were disheartened and cynical; which somehow is able
to persuade tens of thousands of skeptical Jews that
this lowly carpenter, this Roman criminal tried for se-
dition and executed, was their Messiah! Even with the
scandalous rumors about His birth, the allegations of
insanity, the charges of His being demon-possessed—
all made by the leading authorities of the day—tens
of thousands of Jews were still persuaded that this same
individual was in fact God Himself! And further, they
were persuaded to quickly abandon or drastically re-
vise virtually all of their most cherished religious institutions![5]

Following the New Testament era, the early church continued to maintain its testimony as to the resurrection of
Christ.

God has made the Lord Jesus Christ the first-fruits by
raising Him from the dead.
                              —Clement of Alexandria, A.D. 96

For I know that after His resurrection also, He was still
possessed of flesh. And I believe that He is so now.
                              —Ignatius, A.D. 105

The remainder of the Psalm makes it clear that Christ
knew His Father would grant to Him all things that He
asked and that His Father would raise Him from the
dead.

—Justin Martyr, A.D. 160

You will also allow that it was in the flesh that Christ
was raised from the dead. For the very same body that
fell in death, and which lay in the sepulcher, did rise
again.

—Tertullian, A.D. 197[6]

The early church faced unbelievable hardship and trial
from both the civil and religious authorities. It is hard to
believe that the church was able to survive and grow if it
had only been built on deceit. No one would ever submit
to torture and death for what they know to be false. No
one would willingly die for a lie.

Those who deny the bodily resurrection of Christ have
several very hard questions to answer. Why, for example,
didn't the Romans and the Jews exhume the body of Jesus
and put an end to Christianity once and for all?

And what about the willingness of the disciples to die
for their belief that Jesus was alive—even after He had
been murdered as a criminal? Some have claimed that
Elvis Presley rose from the dead, but how many would be
willing to die for such a teaching?

But perhaps the most amazing thing about the early
Christian faith is the way it has grown. Without any sword,
other than the spiritual sword of the Word of God, and
without any attempts at intimidating and terrifying op-
ponents by huge armies and warrior prophets, Christianity has spread to every corner of the globe.

Media moguls, entrepreneurs, and "the rich and the famous" have built great empires. Their fame has been disseminated wide and far, but such popularity is easily explainable. The media continually promotes their productions and flashes pictures of their exploits and wealth. This costs millions of dollars. But the early church did not have millions of dollars. Nor did it have radio and television broadcasts, nor libraries, seminaries, mission boards, and denominational agencies willing to promote the cause of Christ.

Jesus Christ WAS Crucified and Died on the Cross

There have been a variety of attempts to show that Jesus was not crucified. Some say that there was a "switch," others say that Jesus simply went into a "swoon" but did not really die. Several considerations back up the biblical account that Jesus Christ was crucified and that He died.

1. In the Roman world, in order to insure the death of the crucified victim, the legs would be broken with a large board or mallet-like instrument so that the victim could not lift himself and exhale. The victim would be asphyxiated as the lungs filled with carbon dioxide. But the Roman soldiers did not break Jesus' legs because they saw that He was already dead (John 19:32–33). Here were "professionals" who knew the difference between a dead person and a live one.

2. Jesus was embalmed with spices and wrapped in embalming bandages in accordance with the customs of the Jews (John 19:39–40). Even if Jesus had been revived from an alleged swoon, it is highly unlikely that He would have had the strength to unwrap the

bandages, roll back the stone, and escape unnoticed. Embalming took time and involved wrapping bandages around the body and limbs while a mixture of myrrh and aloes was thrown in between the bandages and strips of cloth. There was plenty of opportunity to notice if Jesus were still alive, or if the body had been switched.

3. Pilate asked for assurances that Christ really was dead before releasing the body of Jesus for burial (Mark 15:44–45). Pilate did not want anything to happen that would create the appearance that Jesus had been resurrected, for that would give the early Christian movement credibility and empirical evidence for its claims concerning Christ. If Jesus were not dead, or if the body had been switched, Christ could "pretend" to be resurrected. Of course, we know that there was no pretending. The resurrection really happened. But the care that Pilate exercised made a switch impossible.

4. The physical wounds of Jesus were serious enough to cause death. He had been beaten and whipped repeatedly with a scourge the night before the crucifixion. The scourge was a whip with several thongs to which were attached pieces of broken bone and jagged metal. Scourging tore the flesh, produced bleeding from the multiple wounds, severed nerves and tendons, and led to shock. A crown of thorns had been forced upon His head. Jesus was probably in very serious condition even before being put on the cross.

5. A deputation of Jewish leaders requested Pilate to station a guard around the tomb where Jesus was buried (Matt. 27:62–65). Their motive was the fear that the Lord's followers would secretly come and steal

His body in order to make it appear that a resurrection had taken place. Pilate granted their request. But by guarding the tomb in a way that would make human access virtually impossible, the enemies of Christ unwittingly provided weighty evidence for the fact that the tomb was empty by God's own doing.

6. What better way to keep the disciples from entering the tomb to take away the body of Jesus than to put an official Roman seal on the grave? And this is exactly what happened. Matthew 27:66 relates that the Pharisees requested Pilate to set a seal on the grave. The seal was a cord to which was affixed a glob of clay or wax bearing the official insignia of Roman authority. Anyone trying to take the body of Jesus for the purpose of claiming that He had been resurrected would have broken the seal and thus incurred the wrath of Rome. This was a strong deterrent and served to give credence to the truth that the empty tomb was explained only in terms of resurrection.

7. Matthew 28:11–15 relates how the Jewish authorities bribed the Roman guard and asked them to explain the empty tomb by falsely claiming that the disciples had come and taken away Jesus' body. The Jewish authorities promised to protect the guard from any charges of having failed to do their duty. "And if this come to the governor's ears, we will persuade him, and secure you" (Matt. 28:14). Here is an admission that the grave was indeed empty. If it were not empty there would be no need for a plot to explain that it was.

What prompted the Jewish authorities to take this action? "Behold, some of the watch came into the city, and shewed unto the chief priests all the things that were done" (Matt. 28:11). This report probably included mention of the angel, the earthquake, the removal of the stone from the entrance of the tomb, and the breaking of the seal. The Jews may not have believed the report, but one thing is certain: they did not want the general population to hear what the soldiers really had to say.

Did the Crucifixion of Jesus Rob God?

Muslims believe that Allah would never allow Jesus to die on the cross. That Jesus was so treated by angry men who crucified Him on Calvary's cross would be dishonoring to God. How wrong they are! The death of Christ did not dishonor God. To the contrary, by offering His Son as a propitiatory sacrifice for the sins of the world, God could maintain His perfect holiness and justice while at the same time showing mercy and love to the undeserving.

Referring to Jesus Christ, the Bible states: "Whom God hath set forth to be a propitiation through faith in his blood, to declare his righteousness for the remission of sins that are past, through the forbearance of God; To declare, I say, at this time his righteousness: **that he might be just, and the justifier of him which believeth in Jesus**" (Rom. 3:25–26). All of this means that we have an honorable pardon, through the grace and mercy of God. Because Muslims don't have a cross, or a covenant, or the blood of Christ, they can only have a religion of good works and human effort. Salvation depends on their effort and strength.

A reading of the Koran will make it evident that Allah is a deity of incredible power. But where is his love? Does he identify with his people or does he burden them with burdens that they cannot bear? Has Allah ever conde-

scended to live with people, or does he continue to re-
main distant and out of reach, wrapped in a cloud of in-
approachability?

There is a story told about a group of Holocaust prisoners. On a cold winter afternoon, the prisoners returned
to camp from a work detail. They noticed that a gallows
had been erected in the middle of camp.

The guards instructed all of the prisoners to gather
around. Then the commander went through the crowd
of shivering prisoners. He pointed to one man and motioned him to come forward. Then the commander pointed at another man to come forward. The guard looked
around for a few seconds, then pointed to a little boy and
motioned him to come forward. They were all to be hung
until dead.

The guards placed the first man on a chair and put
the noose around the man's neck. After a tense moment,
the guard kicked the chair from under the man's feet. He
died instantly. The guard did the same thing with the
second man. He, too, died instantly. Then the guard put
the little boy on the chair, and put the noose around his
neck and kicked the chair out from under his feet.

But the boy did not die. He was too light of weight
and the rope did not break his neck. The boy was gag-
ging and kicking, and the boy's mother begged the guard
to shoot him and put him out of his misery. The guard
refused.

A voice in the crowd of prisoners was heard to say:
"You say there is a God? Why doesn't He do something?
Where is God?"

A man in the front of the crowd stepped forward and
pointed to the boy. "He is there, hanging at the end of
that rope."

When Jesus was crucified, it looked like a defeat for God. The disciples were thoroughly disappointed and thought that all was lost. But at that very moment in time God was indeed doing something and working marvelously. He was there, on the cross.

The Death of Christ and the Glory of God

The death of Christ did not rob God the Father of anything, nor was He insulted. He *allowed* Christ to die. It

was part of the plan of grace. "He is despised and rejected of men; a man of sorrows, and acquainted with grief. . . . Yet it pleased the LORD to bruise him; he hath put him to grief" (Isa. 53:3,10).

It is no unusual or great thing for God to condemn a sinner for his or her sins. This is what strict justice demands, and God is a God of justice. The real marvel is that God *provided* the sacrifice to pay for the sins of the world.

It would be wrong to conclude that the cross was first necessary if God were to love a lost and sinful humanity. That is untrue. God already loved a lost and sinful humanity prior to the death of Christ on the cross. "For God so loved the world that he gave . . ." (John 3:16).

Without a cross, and without a covenant, and without blood there can be no intimacy between God and man. One can examine all of the ninety-nine names for Allah, and it will be found that even the most faithful and devout Muslim refers to Allah only as servant to master. While some of the titles of Allah imply goodness on the part of Allah, and may also call him the "merciful," mercy is redefined: "Allah is merciful because he has not killed me."

The Caner brothers, former Muslims who are now seminary professors, write that Allah is "The Cold Judge."

Islam . . . looks to a god of the scales, as opposed to the atoning God the Son. Allah forgives only at the repentance of the Muslim, and all consequences for sin and the debt of guilt fall on the Muslim, who comes to Allah in terror, hoping for a commutation of his sentence. Allah is a "Liberal Giver," (Al-Wahab) but with the character of a fierce warrior who decides to be merciful in response to victory. Again, one sees a judge, as opposed to a God of love.[7]

Chapter Three
Muhammad and His
Followers on the Trinity

Muslims claim that the oneness of God is what makes Islam unique. In the booklet *Just One Message*, we read: "Indeed, this message concerning the Oneness of God (i.e., *tawheed* in Arabic) is the *essential theme* of the Qur'an." The author affirms, "This one true God is ONE, *not three or more!* He has no partners."

The biblical concept of the Triunity of God seems ridiculous to Muslims. The author of the above booklet challenges Christians and asks: "What do you mean by saying that GOD is ONE, while you refer to THREE GODS? Is God ONE in THREE or THREE in ONE (1 in 3 or 3 in 1)?!" he asks. And then, proud of his imagined victory over the Christian the author asks: "By the way, if Jesus, God the Son (or Son of God) is really God or part of the one God, doesn't this contradict what the Bible itself reports that no one can see God, nor hear His voice?"

The difficulty is only apparent. There is no contradiction. God took upon Himself full humanity without ceasing to be God. Jesus Christ is One person with two natures, something that became a reality after the incarnation. In Exodus 33:20 God said to Moses, "Thou canst not see my face: for there shall no man see me, and live." This refers to God prior to the incarnation and does not contradict the Deity of Jesus Christ, nor does it contradict anything else in the Bible.

There is nothing in the later biblical revelation that would support the Muslim claim that there is some kind of a contradiction here, either. John 1:18 states, "No man hath seen God at any time." This means that no man has seen God the Father at any time. It does not deny that people can see God the Son.

Moreover, the Bible never teaches that no one can hear God's voice. Exodus 20:1 states: "And God spake all these words, saying . . ." and then follows the Ten Commandments.

In this chapter we will look at Muslim misperceptions regarding what the Bible teaches and why these misperceptions cause them to misunderstand Christian teaching on the Triune nature of God.

Muslims Don't Understand the Doctrine of the Trinity

Islam erroneously conceives of trinitarianism as tritheism—belief in three gods. It also sees the Christian doctrine of the Deity of Christ as the deification of a man—as in the case of the ancient Romans who deified their emperors—when, in fact, that is not at all the case. The biblical doctrine concerning Christ is not that man became God, but rather that God became man without ceasing to be God.

Since this is such a burning issue, many Christians feel intimidated by Muslims who ask, "Do you believe in the Trinity?" If the Christian says "yes," the Muslim will charge him with tri-theism. If the Christian says "no," he will have denied an essential doctrine of the Christian faith. We must affirm our belief in the Trinity, but we must define what we mean by the term.

Based on Surah 5:116 of the Koran, Muslims have been led to believe that, according to Christian teaching, the three persons of the Godhead are God, Jesus, and Mary. This is certainly not what Christian theology teaches.

The Koran asserts that Allah has "no partners" or "offspring." There is good reason to believe that this was directed not primarily against Christian trinitarianism, but against Arab polytheism that flourished on the pre-Islamic Arabian peninsula. The Koran refers to the three favorite deities of the Meccans: Lat, Uzza, and Manat who were revered as "the three daughters of Allah." This suggests that the koranic teachings denying that God has "partners" or "offspring" was not directed against orthodox Christian teaching but against "the polytheistic idea of Allah's paternity of the Meccan pantheon."[8]

By "Trinity" we do not mean that the Godhead is composed of three separate individuals, like Matthew, Mark, and Luke. Such would create the impression that we believe in three gods, which is tri-theism, not trinitarianism. Nor do we mean that the Godhead is just one person who manifests himself in different modes of existence, as Father, Son, and Holy Spirit—which is modalism and which Christianity denies.

Some Muslims are like Jehovah's Witnesses and will argue that the word "Trinity" is not even in the Bible, and therefore we believe something that is not in the Bible. However, we ought to make the point with the Muslim that the Arabic word for the oneness of God (*tawheed*) is not in the Koran, either.[9] No doubt, the Koran does teach the concept of Allah's *tawheed*, though not using the word, just as the Bible teaches the trinitarian nature of God without using the term "Trinity."

Gary Redman is correct when he states, "Ultimately, Islam rejects the Trinity not out of any supposed rational arguments, but because what it believes is divine revelation rejects that which it (wrongly) imagines the Trinity to mean."[10]

Reducing God to Fit the Human Mind

Muslims claim that the doctrine of the Trinity is irrational and unreasonable, yet they talk about the incomprehensibility of Allah. Here are several statements about the incomprehensibility of Allah.

And thus it is clear and certain—as Islam emphatically proclaims—that He is infinitely beyond anything which the mind or sense of man can grasp or comprehend or imagine or explain. . . .

But to have complete knowledge of God is beyond man's ability. Man is finite and Allah is infinite. . . . The creature cannot comprehend the Creator. . . .

Islam preaches that mankind should only refer to Allah as He has referred to Himself. There is no scope whatsoever for inventing new ideas about Him or thinking of Him in a manner that suits us.

Christian trinitarianism likewise teaches that God cannot be exhaustively known. God is far beyond our frail minds. Even the greatest intellects cannot fathom or probe deeply the mysteries of God. The Muslim claim that the Trinity is unreasonable is a claim that is itself unreasonable.

> Muslims frequently accuse the Christian concept of the Trinity as being inconceivable to reason. Yet, if God is transcendent and accessible only through self-revelation, it follows that the Christian dogma *is* indeed credible. The Muslim position indicates that if we could comprehend God, He would not be God, and that all human attempts to comprehend Him apart from Revelation are inadequate and doomed to failure. This is indeed the Christian position."[11]

In dialoguing with the Muslim we must affirm that the God of Scripture cannot be understood exhaustively by the finite human mind. We must also point out that we are not asking the Muslim to abandon his monotheism. We are simply asking him to consider that he may have denied the incomprehensibility of God in his arguments against the Trinity. Does he really believe that God is incomprehensible? The following illustration will suffice.

Augustine, the early church father, was walking along a beach one day and meditating on the mystery of the Trinity. He observed a little boy running to the sea, filling up a bucket, and pouring the contents of the bucket into a hole in the sand. Augustine inquired of the boy as to what he was doing. The boy said, "I am trying to put the ocean into this hole." Augustine realized that the boy was trying to do what was impossible. Then it dawned on him that it was also impossible to pour all the truth of God's being into a finite mind.

What Scripture Teaches

Scripture shows that the title of "God" is applied to each of the Persons within the Godhead. Peter writes to the saints and refers to them as those who are "elect according to the  foreknowledge of *God the Father*" (1 Pet. 1:2). In Hebrews 1:8, God the Father speaks of Jesus and says, "Thy throne, *O God*, is for ever and ever." In Acts 5:3–4, it is stated that lying to the Holy Spirit is the same as lying to God.

Scripture also speaks of all three Persons of the Godhead as having the attributes of Deity.

- *Omnipresence*—The Father, the Son and the Holy Spirit are spoken of as being present in all places (Matt. 19:26; 28:18–20; Ps. 139:7).
- *Omniscience*—The Father, the Son and the Holy Spirit possess the attribute of being all-knowing (Rom. 11:33; Matt. 9:4; 1 Cor. 2:10).
- *Omnipotence*—All three Persons are spoken of as having all power—the Father (1 Pet. 1:5); the Son (Matt. 28:18), and the Holy Spirit (Rom. 15:19).

Not only do all of the Divine Persons have the attributes of Deity, but they do the works of Deity, such as the creation of all things. This is said of: the Father (Gen. 2:7; Ps. 104:5); the Son (John 1:3; Col. 1:16; Heb. 1:2); and the Holy Spirit (Gen. 1:2; Job 33:4; Ps. 104:30).

God Is Triune

The Bible is trinitarian throughout. It presupposes that God is triune. In fact, even when the Bible is not speaking about the Trinity it nevertheless reveals the triune nature of God in several ways.

In the Hebrew Old Testament there are different words indicating "one." There is the word *yachid,* which means a unitary oneness, something like the Islamic concept of *tawheed.* In Psalm 68:6 *yachid* refers to the solitary person who is alone. Muslims should expect that this is the word used of God in the Hebrew Old Testament. However, such is not the case.

When describing God, the Bible uses the Word *echad,* a word referring to a composite unity. In order to make the point, let's look at how *echad* is used.

Remember This

     ◆ Genesis 2:24: Adam and Eve became one *(echad)* flesh (a composite unity consisting of husband and wife).

     ◆ Genesis 3:22: Adam and Eve had become as one *(echad)* in their knowledge of good and evil (though this knowledge involved two persons).

     ◆ Genesis 34:16,22: The Shechemites wanted to become "one" *(echad)* with the Jews though more than one person was involved.

     ◆ 2 Chronicles 30:12: God gave the people "one *(echad)* heart" though more than one person was involved.

It is clear that *echad* is used in reference to a composite unity, while *yachid* is not. But which "one" is used to describe God? We will start with the Old Testament *Shema,* the classic Old Testament passage recited by Jews to emphasize their monotheistic faith. "Hear, O Israel: The LORD our God is one LORD"(Deut. 6:4).

The Hebrew word translated "one"is *echad.* It could be translated "the LORD our God is one composite unity." Or, "the LORD our God is one Triune Being."

What do Muslims do with this evidence for the triunity of God? They claim that the scribes changed the real Word of God. Can't you just see all of the ancient Jewish scribes feverishly finding all of the manuscripts and changing *yachid* into *echad* to bring about a trinitarian conspiracy and changing hundreds of other scriptures as well?

There are other indirect references to the Trinity. In several scriptures, plural pronouns are used with reference to God.

1. "And the LORD God said, Behold, the man is become as one of **us** . . ." (Gen. 3:22).
2. "And God said, Let **us** make man in **our** image, after **our** likeness . . ." (Gen. 1:26).
3. "Go to, let **us** go down, and there confound their language . . ." (Gen. 11:7).

In number two above, "make" is a plural verb. Indeed, the main verb as well as the pronouns are all plural. These plurals must refer to God, not to God and the angels, because man is not created in two images and likenesses—that of God and that of the angels.

In number three above, "go to" and "confound" are likewise plurals. This, plus the usage of "us," makes it clear that angels are not coming down with God to confound their language. Indeed, no angels are mentioned in the context.

Some anti-trinitarians have tried to argue that these plural references to God are really a "plural of majesty," as when a king or a queen will speak with authority and will therefore use the plural. The example cited is that of Queen Victoria who would say, "**We** are not pleased by these developments."

However, while the plural of majesty is used by kings and queens in modern times, it was not regularly used in the ancient world.

• Genesis 41:41: "And Pharaoh said unto Joseph, See, *I* have set thee over all the land of Egypt."
• Daniel 3:28–29: "Then Nebuchadnezzar spake, and said . . . Therefore *I* make a decree, That every people, nation and language, which speak any thing amiss against the God of Shadrach, Meshach, and Abednego, shall be cut in pieces. . . ."
• Ezra 1:2: "Thus saith Cyrus king of Persia, the LORD God of heaven hath given **me** all the kingdoms of the earth; and he hath charged **me** to build him an house at Jerusalem. . . ."
• Esther 8:7: "Then the king Ahasuerus said unto Esther the queen and to Mordecai the Jew, Behold, **I** have given Esther the house of Haman, and him they have hanged. . . ."

The Trinitarian Wording of
the Great Commission

In Matthew 28:19 we read: "Go ye therefore, and teach all nations, baptizing them in the name of the Father, and of the Son, and of the Holy Ghost." It is significant to note what Jesus does not say:

1. "Baptizing them into the names [plural] of the Father, Son and Holy Spirit," as if there were three names for the same Divine being.
2. "Baptizing them in the name of the Father, and into the name of the Son, and into the name of the Holy Spirit," as if there were three gods, i.e., tritheism.

3. "Baptizing them in the name of the Father, Son and Holy Spirit," omitting the recurring definite article ("the") and therefore supporting the ancient heresy of modalism.

The way the Great Commission is presented in Scripture asserts the unity of the three Divine Persons by combining the Persons under the designation "name," but also showing the uniqueness of each by introducing them with the repeated definite article.

The Church Councils Didn't Invent the Trinity

Some will contend that the church councils "invented" the Trinity for some devious reason. Allegedly it was the Council of Nicea (A.D. 325), or maybe the Council of Constantinople (A.D. 381), or even some later council that came up with the idea. According to those who argue in this fashion, the Trinity is a result of the corruption and paganization of Christianity.

However, those who argue this way have confused the biblical roots of the doctrine with its later creedal expressions. That's something like saying that gravity was invented by Isaac Newton. Newton didn't "invent" gravity, but he did explain it and define it. Morey makes an important point when he writes:

> New terminology for the Trinity was developed and more precise definitions given as various heresies arose which challenged it. But the liberals forget one irrefutable fact. *In order for the doctrine of the Trinity to be defined and defended against the heretics who were attacking it, it obviously had to already exist.* After all, the early heretics were challenging *something*! They

were clearly challenging doctrines that were already in existence. They were objecting to what the Church *already* believed.[12]

These are important scriptures, but we have only touched on a small portion of them. There is nothing like the Trinity in the natural world. Though there have been many illustrations concocted, they all fall far short. This suggests that the Trinity is not a human invention, but a concept revealed by God.

Jesus Is God

> . . . and his name shall be called . . . The mighty God. . . .
> —Isa. 9:6

Though Muslims claim to honor Christ, the Muslim view of Jesus fails to do justice to what Scripture teaches. In Isaiah 9:6 we read: "For unto us a child is born, unto us a son is given: and the government shall be upon his shoulder: and his name shall be called Wonderful, Counsellor, The mighty God, The everlasting Father, the Prince of Peace." Orthodox Jews claim this is a reference to Hezekiah. Muslims claim it's a conspiracy. The Bible claims Jesus is God.

There were several individuals in New Testament times who were considered divine. This was not, however, endorsed by God. When Herod accepted honor from his subjects as being divine, he was eaten alive by worms (Acts 12:23). But in contrast, when Paul and Barnabas were given the honors of divinity, they objected and preached on the One who is the true and living God (Acts 14:11–18). Likewise, Jesus Christ received worship of men and did not rebuke these men, nor did He deny His Divine prerogatives. Indeed, He affirmed that it is the Father's will "that all men should honour the Son, even as they honour the Father" (John 5:23).

Chapter Four

Muhammad and His Followers on Human Rights

In the tract *Human Rights In Islam,* the author asserts that Islam, from its very beginning, has pioneered the concept of human rights. "In the address which the Prophet delivered on the occasion of the Farewell Hijj, he said: 'Your lives and properties are forbidden to one another till you meet your Lord on the Day of Resurrection.' The Prophet has also said about the *dhimmis* (the non-Muslim citizens of the Muslim state): 'One who kills a man under a covenant (i.e. *dhimmi*) will not even smell the fragrance of Paradise.'"

Here the Muslim apologist is showing that even non-Muslims are afforded a high degree of protection. Those who would murder a non-Muslim *dhimmi* will never make it to Paradise. But what is a *dhimmi*?

A *dhimmi* is a non-Muslim subject under an Islamic ruler. *Dhimmis* are members of tolerated minorities but who, in order to stay alive, have to pay the *jizya*—a special tax for being in the "wrong" religion. President George W. Bush is a Methodist. Would we think him to be most gracious and highly charitable if he allowed Baptists protection of life and limb *if they paid a special tax?* The answer is obvious.

The Muslim apologist also indicates that Islam gives everyone the right to protest against tyranny. There is, however, a catch. Since Islam believes that all power comes from Allah, Allah's will determines what is tyranny. The author of the above-cited tract writes: "This was acknowledged by Hazrat Abu Bakr who said in his very first address: 'Cooperate with me when I am right but correct me when I commit error; obey me so long as I follow the commandments of Allah and His prophet; but turn away from me when I deviate.'"

Abu Bakr is speaking about a religious state that is under the rule of Islam. As long as he follows "the commandments of Allah and His prophet" he is above reproach. By this definition, tyranny instigated by those who follow "the commandments of Allah and His prophet" is, by definition, *not tyranny.* Those who persecute the followers of other religions in accordance with the Koran are simply following "the commandments of Allah and His prophet," and are not guilty of tyranny or any other crime.

Imagine what would happen if America became an Islamic nation. The Koran, not the U.S. Constitution would be the "law of the land." How would a Christian, or a Jew, or a Hindu, or a Buddhist, or a Sikh, or an atheist be treated? Or, how would you be treated if you were a

Muslim but did not agree with the ruler's interpretation of a particular passage in the Koran? Would you rest at ease knowing that there is no tyranny under an Islamic ruler?

In another tract, *Moral System of Islam,* we read: "Islam has laid down some universal fundamental rights for humanity as a whole, which are to be observed and respected under all circumstances."

In the same tract, we are further advised that the Koran and Sunnah teach that the faithful Muslim not only has obligations to parents and relatives, but to the entire world. "For example, hunting of birds and animals for the sake of game is not permitted. Similarly, cutting trees and plants which yield fruit is forbidden unless there is a very pressing need for it."

There can be no doubt that before facing the many challenges created by the Meccans and the rejection of the Jews and Christians who came to believe that he was not a prophet of God, Muhammad had a softer side. Muhammad, however, was deeply offended when the Jews rejected his prophetic claims. Islamic specialist Karen Armstrong writes:

> In the early years at Medina there were two important developments. Muhammad had been greatly excited by the prospect of working closely with the Jewish tribes, and had even, shortly before the *hirjah,* introduced some practices (such as communal prayer on Friday afternoons, when Jews would be preparing for the Sabbath, and a fast on the Jewish Day of Atonement) to align Islam more closely to Judaism. His disappointment, when the Jews of Medina refused to accept him as an authentic prophet, was one of the great-

est of his life . . . the polemic with the Jews at Medina occupies a significant proportion of the Quran and shows that it troubled Muhammad.[13]

Though there may have been a softer side to Muhammad, it certainly did not continue to manifest itself in his life nor in the lives of his followers. The following is a brief history of Islamic fundamentalism in the twentieth century. Those who claim that Islam has advanced human rights have to give a credible explanation of the following.

Remember This

• **January 1979**—The Shah of Iran, Mohammed Reza Pahlavi, who had ruled for almost forty years, flees his country as the people demonstrate, demanding an end to his government. The people accuse him of being a despot and of betraying the laws of Islam. The leader of the revolt is an elderly religious leader, Ayatollah Ruhollah Khomeini, who announces the end of the monarchy and the beginning of the Islamic Republic of Iran.

In the late summer of this year, American president Jimmy Carter allows the ailing Shah to enter the U.S. for medical treatment. Furious over this and the long-standing U.S. support of the Shah, Iranian revolutionaries seize the U.S. embassy in Tehran, Iran's capital, and take fifty-three American hostages. The revolutionaries demand that the U.S. hand over the Shah to face trial. The U.S. refuses and the crisis erupts into a rise of anti-U.S. sentiments in the Muslim world. The hostility is fueled by America's support for Israel.

• **October 1981**—Anwar Sadat, the president of Egypt, is assassinated by soldiers from his own army. His assassins claim that they were punishing Sadat, who had violated the tenets of Islam. Sadat had recently met with Israeli officials and was making overtures to the U.S. This assassination was to serve as a warning to moderate Islamic leaders who would court the favor of Israel and the West.

• **February 1989**—A non-practicing Muslim born in India, and a citizen of Britain, by the name of Salman Rushdie, is condemned to die because his novel, *The Satanic Verses,* is thought to be insulting to the Prophet Muhammad and other important individuals in the Islamic faith.

• **February 1993**—A massive bomb blast rips through the basement of the World Trade Center complex in New York City killing six and injuring more than a thousand. The attack is traced to Egyptian immigrants who are followers of Sheikh Omar Abdel-Rahman, a blind Islamic cleric. According to testimony given at the trial, the men involved were seeking revenge against the Egyptian government for its repression of Islamic fundamentalism. This involved attacking the backer of Egypt, the United States.[14]

Anti-Islamic "Propaganda" Propagandized

Those who speak about Islam and its violent past are making baseless accusations and comments, or so we are told. The booklet *The Sword of Islam* tries to convince the reader that this sword is not of steel. "As for the propaganda that it was the sword of steel, that is, force which was instrumental in the universal expansion of Islam, we give below quotations from the writing of some of the prominent non-Muslim scholars and leaders refuting this baseless accusation." In an attempt to refute "this baseless accusation," there follows several quotes from well-known leaders around the world.

- James A Michener: "No other religion in history spread so rapidly as Islam. . . . The West has widely believed that this surge of religion was made possible by the sword. But no modern scholar accepts that idea, and the Qur'an is explicit in support of the freedom of conscience."

- Edward Gibbon: "The greatest success of Mohammad's life was effected by sheer moral force without the stroke of a sword."

- M. K. Gandhi: ". . . I became more than ever convinced that it was not the sword that won a place for Islam in those days in the scheme of life. It was the rigid simplicity, the utter self-effacement of the prophet, the scrupulous regard for his pledges, his intense devotion to his followers, his intrepidity, his fearlessness, his absolute trust in God and his own mission. . . ."

Following these quotations, we read this statement addressed to the reader:

If you too possess a soft, tender heart and an open mind, do write to us for some basic information about the way of life called "Islam." Do not believe in hearsay and learn from the direct sources. We are ready to help.

We are sorry to disagree with such sweet-sounding statements. Islam has advanced through the sword and it is seeking at the present hour to advance through the sword.

The author of this tract must believe that his readers are mentally defective and have the intelligence of a little child.

It would have been far better if the author had written something like: "While it is true that there have been Muslim advances through the use of the sword, every advance has not been violent." Or if he wrote: "While it is true that Islam has advanced through warfare, we believe that warfare is not intrinsic to Islam."

The boldness of the above lies cast a dark shadow on the integrity and credibility of those who would write such a tract which is so obviously designed to deceive. While the individuals quoted as giving their approval to Islam may have been well-intentioned, the author of the tract is being less than honest in using their statements.

More Propaganda at Home

One of the emphases of the "Million-Man March" held on October 16, 1995, as thousands of African-Americans gathered on the Mall in Washington, D.C., was human rights. One author writes that "they came to pledge an end to 'black-on-white' violence, and to renew their commitment to women, children, family, and church—and to political activism for African Americans."[15]

The leader of the Nation of Islam, Louis Farrakhan, spoke for more than two hours. He exhorted his audience to "become totally organized people." He urged them to "become a part of some organization that is working for the uplift of our people. . . . Get back to the houses of God. Be more like Jesus, more like Muhammad, more like Moses." Then thousands of African-American men joined hands and recited the pledge on which the march was founded:

I pledge that from this day forward I will strive to love my brother as I love myself. . . . I pledge that from this day forward I will never raise my hand with a knife or gun to beat, cut, shoot any members of my family or any human being except in self-defense. . . . I will never abuse my wife by striking her, disrespecting her, for she is the mother of my children and the producer of my future.[16]

Yet Farrakhan and the march had many critics who pointed out that Farrakhan's record contradicted his words. "As the head of the Nation of Islam, Farrakhan had frequently railed against the wickedness of whites and their institutions. Indeed, the Nation of Islam itself was a movement traditionally steeped in loathing for the 'white devil' who had, thousands of years ago, the Nation held, subjugated and enslaved blacks."

The Nation of Islam has historically held a belief in "black supremacy," and has also sided with the proponents of anti-Semitism. Farrakhan claimed that the Million-Man March was a "Day of Atonement," the name of the Jewish holy day of fasting and prayer, but this title was offensive to some. "Were these words said by someone else," asserted a Jewish leader, "it would be easier to accept them as a positive tribute to Jewish observance."[17]

The PR Blitz

Islamic propaganda is not only being disseminated through booklets and tracts but also through television. A two-hour PBS documentary was aired in December of 2002 on the life of Muhammad. It was expressly intended to counter the negative images of Muslims that many Americans have.

"Americans get most of their images about Islam and Muslims from the headlines. Demonstrations and shouting in the streets makes the news, and those images are repeated," stated the producer, Alex Kronemer. Who is Alex Kronemer? According to the *Washington Times* he is "an American convert to Islam with a master's degree in theology from Harvard University." Kronemer partnered with Michael Wolfe in the documentary, who is also a convert to Islam.

Kronemer and Wolfe joined with filmmaker Michael Schwartz, who recently went on record as stating that he was amazed "by the numerous affinities between basic American values and core Islamic beliefs," and that the production was targeting "a predominantly non-Muslim American audience." Daniel Pipes, director of the Middle East Forum and author of *Militant Islam Reaches America,* stated that a preliminary examination of the production led him to conclude that "all of this suggests that the American taxpayer is subsidizing an attempt to proselytize Islam in America."[18]

"Affinities Between Basic American Values and Core Islamic Beliefs"?

Filmmaker Schwartz, by his words quoted above, evidently thinks that Muslims can and will be good American citizens. A former Muslim from the Middle East interviewed on our "Watchman  **Land of the Free** on the Wall" broadcast gives several reasons why it is impossible for a Muslim to be a loyal American citizen.

> It's impossible theologically, because his allegiance is to Allah, the moon god of Arabia.
>
> It's impossible scripturally, because of his allegiance to the five pillars of Islam and the Koran.

It is impossible geographically, because his allegiance is to Mecca, to which he turns in prayer five times a day.

It's impossible socially, because his allegiance to Islam demands that he make no friends of Christians and Jews (The Koran, 5:51).

It's impossible politically, because he must submit to the *mullah,* who teaches the annihilation of Israel and the destruction of America, the "Great Satan."

It's impossible domestically, because he is instructed to marry four women and beat and scourge his wife when she disobeys him (The Koran, 4:34).

It's impossible religiously, because no other religion is accepted by his Allah except Islam, which is totally intolerant (The Koran, 2:256).

It's impossible intellectually, because he cannot accept the American Constitution since it is established on biblical principles and he believes the Bible to be corrupt.

It's impossible philosophically, because Islam, Muhammad, and the Koran do not allow freedom of religion and expression. Democracy and Islam cannot coexist. Every Muslim government is dictatorial or autocratic except Turkey.

It's impossible spiritually, because when we declare "one nation under God," the Christian's God is the triune God, while the Muslim's is one entity called "Allah," who is never a heavenly Father, nor is he ever called "Love" in the ninety-nine excellent names.[19]

A Sad Story From Egypt

As reported by an Egyptian pastor, there is widespread discrimination against Christians in Egypt. Christians cannot take advanced studies in the field of medicine and very few can be surgeons, gynecologists, or cardiologists. In the state-operated teachers' college, the Egyptian government allows only five percent of the applicants to be Christian.

In Egypt, churches cannot be built or even remodeled unless permission is obtained from the president. According to this pastor, "Muslim police officers and governors think that Allah will forgive their sins in their eternal paradise when they persecute Christians here on earth."

In the city of El Mina, the secret police destroyed one church restroom because the church did not get permission to remodel it. A request for such permission can take five years, but if someone wishes to build a mosque, the government will allow construction to begin immediately and provide utilities free of charge.[20]

Does anyone really believe that Muhammad and his followers have advanced human rights? Does anyone really believe that if America became an Islamic nation, the situation in America would be any different than it is in Egypt at the present time?

Why are leaders and government officials repeatedly ignoring the evidence? Is the administration afraid of being offensive to the Arab Middle East and not winning support for a war against Middle Eastern tyrants? Or is it concern about the oil supply?

If this is the case, it is a moral travesty—and it is foolish strategically. America cannot win the favor of Muslims in the Middle East and elsewhere by ignoring the cries of the oppressed and tiptoeing around evil.

President Bush on Islam

America is a nation that seeks to be religiously neutral in

the sense that no one religion is endorsed or discriminated against. As the leader of a pluralistic nation, President Bush finds himself in the position of being the president of American Muslims as well as American Christians. His profession of Christianity means that he has to overcome a natural barrier that people of other faiths might experience since his faith is different than theirs. Moreover, he has the difficult position of trying to win, or at least keep, our allies in the Middle East. The president has sought to make it clear that America's war on terrorism is not a war against Islam.

From all of this, it is clear that Mr. Bush is in a very difficult situation. The reader is therefore encouraged to pray for the president, as well as all of our leaders, as instructed by the apostle in 1 Timothy 2:1–2: "I exhort therefore, that, first of all, supplications, prayers, intercessions, and giving of thanks, be made for all men; For kings, and for all that are in authority; that we may lead a quiet and peaceable life in all godliness and honesty."

In an effort to keep lines of communication open, the president has made several comments about Islam. The following is but a sampling.

- The president's remarks on U.S. humanitarian aid to Afghanistan at the Presidential Hall, Dwight David Eisenhower Executive Office Building, Washington, D.C., October 11, 2002:

> Islam is a vibrant faith. Millions of our fellow citizens are Muslim. We respect the faith. We honor its traditions. Our enemy does not. Our enemy doesn't follow the great traditions of Islam. They hijacked a great religion.

Islam is a faith that brings comfort to people. It inspires them to lead lives based on honesty and justice and compassion.

• Presidential remarks at a Roundtable discussion with Arab-and Muslim-American leaders, Afghanistan Embassy, Washington, D.C., September 10, 2002:

All Americans must recognize that the face of terror is not the true faith . . . of Islam. It is a faith that brings comfort to a billion people around the world. It's a faith that has made brothers and sisters of every race. It's a faith based upon love, not hate.

• Presidential remarks as Mr. Bush called for new Palestinian leadership, the Rose Garden, Washington, D.C., June 24, 2002:

If liberty can blossom on the rocky soil of the West Bank and Gaza, it will inspire millions of men and women around the globe who are equally weary of poverty and oppression, equally entitled to the benefits of democratic government. I have a hope for the people of Muslim countries. Your commitments to morality, and learning, and tolerance led to great historical achievements. And those values are alive in the Islamic world today. You have a rich culture, and you share the aspirations of men and women in every culture. Prosperity and freedom and dignity are not just American hopes, or Western hopes. They are universal, human hopes. And even in the violence and turmoil of the Middle East, America believes these hopes have the power to transform lives and nations.

• Remarks made by President Bush at Iftaar dinner, the State Dining Room, Washington, D.C., November 19, 2001:

According to Muslim teachings, God first revealed His word in the Holy Qur'an to the prophet Muhammad, during the month of Ramadan. That word has guided billions of believers across the centuries, and those believers built a culture of learning and literature and science. All the world continues to benefit from this faith and its achievements.

• President Bush's remarks made in his "Message for Ramadan," November 15, 2001:

The Islam that we know is a faith devoted to the worship of one God, as revealed through the Holy Qur'an. It teaches the value and the importance of charity, mercy, and peace.

• President Bush's remarks to His Majesty King Abdullah of Jordan, the Oval Office, Washington, D.C., September 28, 2001:

I have assured His majesty that our war is against evil, not against Islam. There are thousands of Muslims who proudly call themselves Americans, and they know what I know—that the Muslim religion is based upon peace and love and compas-

sion. The exact opposite of the teachings of the al-
Qaeda organization, which is based upon evil and
hate and destruction.[21]

There are several books that have been written which
have investigated whether or not Islam is a religion of
peace. I have authored a book entitled *Religion of Peace
or Refuge for Terror?* which is available through Southwest Radio Church Ministries, 1-800-652-1144.

Some Christians have strong reservations about President Bush's comments about Islam. These comments are
driving a wedge between conservative Christians and the
president. Evangelist Pat Robertson, for example, expressed dissatisfaction with President Bush, who visited
a Washington, D.C. mosque on December 5, 2002, and
praised Muslims who "lead lives of honesty, integrity and
morality." Robertson called Islam "violent to the core"
and said that the president should refrain from religious
commentary, as he "is not elected as chief theologian."[22]

Others have pointed out that despite the numerous
indications of the high likelihood of further attacks on
American soil, the U.S. government and the news media
are unwilling to acknowledge the dangerous religious
motivations behind the current conflict. As expert Mid-
east analyst Daniel Pipes has stated: "A virtual taboo ex-
ists in official circles about Islam's role in the violence; in
the words of one senior State Department official, this
subject 'has to be tiptoed around.'"[23]

Many experts agree that Islam is more than a religion
of high moral teachings. In fact, "the heart of Islamic
teaching is that religion is not just a part of life, but life is
a tiny part of religion. Thus everything in life is dominat-
ed by this religion. As such Islam is a system. It is a socio-

political, socio-religious, socio-economical, educational, legislative, judicial, and militaristic system garbed in religious terminology."[24]

Islam and the American Way of Life

While it is true that Islam is not monolithic, it is also true that all of Islam leans in the direction of religious authoritarianism that puts its deity

Land of the Free before the needs of a free society.

> . . . there is one common feature of Islamism as it assumes power: an irresistible leaning toward authoritarianism. The explanation, again, lies in Islamist thought: Islamists share the idea that God, not the people, is sovereign, and that obedience to God, not the rights of man, must be the governing principle of a just state. The role of the Islamic state is not to legislate the will of the people, but to implement the will of God.[25]

In a recent "Watchman on the Wall" interview with this author, Dr. Anis Shorrosh outlined the "Islamic Ten-Year Plan to Take Over America." I share it with the reader, who will be able to readily see these things happening at the present time:

1. Accelerate Islamic demographic growth by: massive immigration; no use of birth control because every baby born of Muslim parents is automatically Muslim; Muslim men marry American women (at present ten thousand annually); convert angry, alienated black prison inmates and turn them into militant Muslims.

2. Manipulate the intelligence community with misinformation to periodically terrorize Americans of impending attacks on bridges, tunnels, water supplies,

power plants, and other facilities, to wear down the American population.

3. Engage the American public in dialogues and debates in colleges and universities and libraries and radio talk shows on the virtues of Islam, and seek to show how Islam is very much like other religions in that Islam promotes noble ideals.

4. Reading, writing, and arithmetic lessons in Islamic schools (there are three hundred of them in America that are exclusively Islamic) should be sprinkled with a dislike of Jews, evangelical Christians, and democracy.

5. Attack America's economy by interfering with the supply of America's black gold—over one thousand products come from oil. This would devastate the economy of America.

6. Control as much of the press—radio, TV, newspapers, internet as possible—by pressuring corporations to buy into the controlling stock.

7. Appeal to the sensitivities of compassionate Americans for sympathy and tolerance of the Muslim minority.

8. Urge Muslims to penetrate the White House and Congress, and by getting involved in government positions, school boards, and so on. Have you ever noticed how numerous Muslim doctors are in America when their own countries need them more desperately than anything else?

9. Sway black leaders like Louis Farrakhan to promote Islam as the original African religion while Christianity is presented as being only for whites.

10. Abandon freedom of speech and replace it with hate-crime bills in the Senate and Congress.

Chapter Five

Muhammad and His Followers on Women's Rights

In order to offset the bad publicity over Islam's treatment of women, Islamic apologists are working doubly hard to convince the world that Islam really has advanced women's rights. Some of the Muslims who make this claim are Muslim women. In a guest column entitled "Women fare well under Islam," we read the following words written by a Muslim woman:

> She holds a degree from one of the nation's most elite universities. She manages her own finances. She keeps her maiden name after marriage. She firmly defends her beliefs. She stands out in defiance of social norms. Who is she? Postmodern feminist clad in a pinstripe Armani power-suit? Not quite. No, she is a Muslim woman, clad in a head scarf. Not quite the answer that you expected, I supposed.

The column continues with: "Contrary to the general public's perception of Muslim women as oppressed, repressed, and submissive, Islam granted women certain rights before they were even a vague dream in the minds of Western women."[26]

After reading this, one wonders how the public *ever* got such a perception of Muslim women. Has there been some terrible conspiracy against Muslims? The answer to this is obvious. The general public's perception of Muslim women has come from Muslim women and the way they are treated. There is a long, undeniable history of abuse against women in Muslim circles.

But what about the statement that "Islam granted women certain rights before they were even a vague dream in the minds of Western women"? Yes, Islam antedates much of European history. When some Europeans were living in very primitive societies Islam had already developed a cultural and religious heritage that has been as sophisticated as any in the West. But cultural and religious sophistication is not a guarantee of women's rights. Moreover, one has to ask: Is the author of this guest column your average Muslim woman? Is she the rule, or is she the exception?

The opening paragraph of the column states that this young lady "stands out in defiance of social norms." This certainly cannot mean defiance of the social norms of the West. Many Western women attend "elite universities, manage their own finances, and firmly defend their beliefs." This woman is defying the social norms of *Islamic culture.* Her defiance contradicts the title of her column, "Women fare well under Islam."[27]

The facts show that women don't fare well under Islam. Former Muslim Ibn Warraq cites the greatly revered

Islamic philosopher, al-Ghazali (1058–1111), who wrote about the woman's role with the following words:

> She should stay at home and get on with her spinning, she should not go out often, she must not be well-informed, nor must she be communicative with her neighbors, and only visit them when absolutely necessary; she should take care of her husband and respect him in his presence and his absence and seek to satisfy him in everything; she must not cheat on him nor extort money from him; she must not leave her house without his permission and if given his permission she must leave surreptitiously. She should put on old clothes and take deserted streets and alleys, avoid markets, and make sure that a stranger does not hear her voice or recognize her; she must not speak to a friend of her husband even in need. . . . Her sole worry should be her virtue, her home as well as her prayers and her fast. If a friend of her husband calls when the latter is absent she must not open the door nor reply to him in order to safeguard her and her husband's honour. She should be clean and ready to satisfy her husband's sexual needs at any moment. . . .[28]

No doubt, someone could find something written by a Christian that sounds very similar. But nations and societies that have been built on Christian principles do not abuse women. The abuse of women is the exception rather than the rule. With Islamic nations it is the rule rather than the exception.

The *Hijab* and *Abaya*

According to Gihan El Gindy, writing in the booklet *Seeing Through The Veil,* the *hijab* can be defined as "the garment used to cover the head with the exception of the face and hands. The *abaya* is defined as the garment used to cover the body with one sheet of cloth pulled over the head."[29] El Gindy states: "Wearing the *hijab* never diminishes a woman's rights. On the contrary, following the Islamic dress code, wearing the *hijab* gives her a better chance at being selected as a wife. . . . In all societies, wearing the *hijab* decreases the chances for possible rape, assault, and/or sexual crimes that are based upon unnecessary physical and sexual exposures."[30]

No doubt, women are to dress modestly, and that is commanded in Scripture (1 Tim. 2:9), but we shouldn't think that the only way a woman can be modest is by following the Islamic dress code for women.

What is it like for a woman to follow the dress code? Sultanna is a Saudi Arabian princess, born into unbelievable wealth. She had four mansions on three continents, her own private jet, glittering jewels, and the best of clothing. Her real life, however, is one of bondage. In the book *Princess: A True Story of Life Behind the Veil In Saudi Arabia,*[31] she tells what it is like to be forced to wear the veil:

I must admit that the first few moments of veiling were exciting. I found the veil a novelty and looked back with interest as Saudi teenage boys stared at me, now a mysterious figure in black. I knew they were wishing for a bit of breeze to blow the veil away from my face so that they might catch a glimpse of my forbidden skin. For a moment, I felt myself a thing of beauty, a work so lovely that I must be covered to protect men from their uncontrollable desires.

The novelty of wearing the veil and *abaya* was fleeting, though. When we walked out of the cool *souq* area into the blazing hot sun, I gasped for breath and sucked furiously through the sheer black fabric. The air tasted stale and dry as it filtered through the thin gauzy cloth. I had purchased the sheerest veil available, yet I felt I was seeing life through a thick screen. How could women see through veils made of a thicker fabric? The sky was no longer blue, the glow of the sun had dimmed; my heart plunged to my stomach when I realized that from that moment, outside my own home I would not experience life as it really is in all its color. The world suddenly seemed a dull place. And dangerous, too! I groped and stumbled along the pitted, cracked sidewalk, fearful of breaking an ankle or leg.[32]

There are several interesting things about Sultana's words. Though Muslim apologists state that Islamic dress protects women, the truth is that it is worn by women to protect *men* from the danger of "their uncontrollable desires."

Why are Muslim women to be so thoroughly covered? A converted Muslim states: "The hair of a woman appearing under her head cover is like an arrow in the heart of a Muslim to fill him with lust—they are protecting the men, not the women. They also cover them up to avoid showing the bruises that the wives have received from their husbands beating them up."[33]

Muhammad and Polygamy

What is it like to be one wife among many? Sultana relates the personal grief she experienced when her husband, Kareem, said he wanted another wife.

"Sultana, I am a man that can afford many children. I

desire ten, twenty, as many as God sees fit to give me."

He paused for what seemed a lifetime. I held my breath in fear.

"Sultana, I am going to wed another. As the second wife, she will be there to provide me children. I need nothing further from her, only children. My love is always with you. . . ."

Kareem waited for my reaction. At first, I could not move. My breath finally came back to me in deep, ragged gasps. The truth of his announcement slowly sank into my mind and came to life; when my strength returned, I could answer him only with a fit of passion that brought us both to the floor.

The depth of my pain could not be expressed in words. I needed to hear Kareem beg for my mercy as I clawed his face . . . and tried desperately to kill the man who was my husband. . . .

I told Kareem that I wanted a divorce; I would never submit to the humiliation of his taking another wife. Kareem replied that divorce would be out of the question unless I chose to give up my children for his second wife to raise. He would never allow them to leave his home.

Kareem could mouth any deception he chose, but I understood the implications of his taking a second wife. The desire for children was not his basis. The issue was primitive. We had been wed for eight years; sexual license was his aim. Obviously, my husband was weary of eating the same dish and sought a new, exotic fare for his palate. . . .[34]

Some Muslim women, such as Sultana, find no fault with Muhammad or with Islam for the way they are treated. They believe the fault lies with the men who followed Muhammad and who corrupted Islam. Sultana, whose account is recorded above, expresses this view when she writes:

It is wrong, however, to blame our Muslim faith for the lowly

position of women in our society. Although the Koran
does state that women are secondary to men, much in
the same way the Bible authorizes men to rule over
women, our Prophet Mohammed taught only kindness
and fairness toward those of my sex. The men who
came behind Prophet Mohammed have chosen to follow the customs and traditions of the Dark Ages rather than to follow Mohammed's words and example.
Our Prophet scorned the practice of infanticide, a com-
mon custom in his day of ridding the family of un-
wanted females. Prophet Mohammed's very words ring
with his concern at the possibility of abuse and indif-
ference toward females: "Whoever hath a daughter,
and doth not bury her alive, or scold her, or prefer his
male children to her, may God bring him into Paradise."[35]

Sultana is being kind, but she is not seeing the whole
picture. It was not "the men who came behind Prophet
Mohammed" and who have followed the "traditions of
the Dark Ages" who taught the legitimacy of multiple
wives, but rather Muhammad himself. While Sultana is
unhappy with multiple wives, Muhammad set the example for his followers. The Koran allows only four wives,
but Muhammad had thirteen or even fifteen. We know
the names of at least eleven.

1. **Khadija**—A rich widow of Mecca whom Muhammad
   married when he was twenty-five and she forty-five.
2. **Sauda**—Khadija died when Muhammad was fifty. He
   married Sauda, who was a widow, and shortly there-
   after he married a third wife.
3. **Aisha**—She was six or seven at the time of the mar-

riage, which was consummated when she was nine.

4. **Hafsa**—There was much rivalry beween Aisha and Hafsa, but the former maintained her supremacy in the Prophet's heart.

5. **Zainab**—Muhammad's adopted son's ex-wife. Muhammad's marriage to Zayd's ex-wife caused a scandal, but Muhammad claimed that it was done by Allah's command. The same Surah (see 33:37,50) allows Muhammad more than four wives.

6. **Juwariyah**—One of the captives in Muhammad's many expeditions for plunder, a woman who was known for her great beauty.

7. **Raihana**—A Jewess captured by Muhammad in his battle against the Quraiza Jews.

8. **Maryam**—An Egyptian-Christian slave girl. The fondness of Muhammad for Maryam was resented by his other wives. To punish them for their attitude, he lived with Maryam alone for a month.

9. **Saffiya**—Muhammad attacked Khaibar, a Jewish settlement on the road to Damascus. Saffiya was one of the captives and was fifteen at the time of marriage.

10. **Um Habeeba**—Not much is known about this wife.

11. **Maimuna of Mecca**—Not much is known about this wife, either.[36]

But what about polygamy in the Bible? Polygamy was never endorsed by God, though it was tolerated. The first mention of a polygamous relationship—Lamech and his wives Adah and Zillah (Gen. 4:19)—is in a context of rebellion against God. The pattern of Genesis 2:24–25— one man and one woman—was reinforced by Jesus when He referred to this latter passage as being the ideal for today (Matt. 19:4–6). In Titus 1:6 a church leader is to be "the husband of one wife." This is a translation of a phrase that literally means "a one-woman man." The monogamous marriage relationship is a picture of the relationship between Christ and His bride, which is the church (Eph. 5:31–32).

Islam and the Oppression of Women

Is there any intrinsic connection between Islam and the oppression of women, or is the oppression of women in Islamic countries merely coincidental? Though many Muslim apologists would deny that there is any connection, the facts don't lie. Women fare poorly under Islam. Don't believe everything you hear. While the purveyors of alcoholic beverages may protest and shout that whiskey-drinkers are a sober-minded lot, known for their noble ideals and intellectual accomplishments, the facts speak for themselves. The same is true with the plight of women in Muslim nations. Nation after nation that is under Islamic law abuses women. This is a fact. There must be, therefore, something endemic to Islam that leads to the abuse of women. What is it? A collection of factors: the Koran, the Hadith, the example of Muhammad and his followers.

> *Husbands, love your wives, even as Christ . . . gave himself for it.*
> —Eph. 5:25

Don't think so? Well answer this question: How many Christian nations practice "honor killings"?

The Human Rights Commission of Pakistan has recently released a report indicating that more than four hundred fifty women were murdered in Pakistan during 2002, all in the name of family honor. In its annual report on human rights in Pakistan, the commission also reported that despite parliamentary elections, "democracy and democratic practices were harshly curbed."

The report explains that the term "honor killings" refers to the practice of murdering a woman, often carried out by her male relatives, for having sexual relations before marriage. "Cases of mutilation of women and burning of their faces and bodies with acid have also increased. Women are often mutilated by their in-laws following family disputes. In some areas, men also throw acid on women when their marriage proposals are turned down."[37]

Strangely enough, even female Muslim apologists seek to justify the koranic restrictions imposed on women. Female intellectuals like Ahmad Jamal, Ms. Zahya Kaddoura, Ms. Ghada al-Kharsa, and Ms. Madiha Khamis find Allah's true wisdom in these passages and argue that they are justified because "women are sensitive, emotional, sentimental, easily moved, and influenced by their biological rhythm." In an Islamic court, because women are allegedly inferior, the testimony of two female witnesses must be sought. Yet, as Ibn Warraq observes, "by taking the testimony of two beings whose reasoning faculties are faulty, we do not obtain the testimony of one complete person with a perfectly functioning rational faculty—such is Islamic arithmetic!"[38]

Equal With Men?

While devious Muslims will claim that women are equal with men under Islam, equality does not mean equal worth and equal rights. Tuffaha states:

> The woman is equal to the man in Islam before the
> law . . . but the woman is not equal to the man with
> regard to her social worth and her subjective rights,

for how can the commanding and the commanded,
the great and the small, the knowledgeable and the
ignorant, the sane and the mad, the unjust and the
just, the honorable and the insignificant, the able and
the unable, the working and the lazy, the strong and
the weak be equal? We must not then mix between
equality before the law and the social worth of the
human being.[39]

This, perhaps, explains the vagaries of Islamic law regarding women. For example Islamic law actually protects
rapists. One former Muslim writes that in order to prove
rape,

Four Muslim adult males of good repute must be
present to testify that sexual penetration has taken
place. Furthermore, in keeping with good Islamic practice, these laws value the testimony of men over wom-
en. The combined effect of these laws is that it is impossible for a woman to bring a successful charge of
rape against a man; instead, she herself, the victim,
finds herself charged with illicit sexual intercourse,
while the rapist goes free. If the rape results in a preg-
nancy, this is automatically taken as an admission that
adultery or fornication has taken place with the woman's consent rather than that rape has occurred.[40]

On the basis of their studies of Islamic history and documents, Rafiqul-Haqq and Newton state that Islam is "consistent in teaching the superiority of men over women."[41]
This means that a husband may treat a rebellious wife
with the most drastic of measures. Such is encouraged by
Surah 4:34, which teaches that a man may beat his rebel-

lious wife and sexually desert her. Sayyed Qotb explains the rationale of this sexual desertion: "The man has to make a superior psychological move against all her attraction and beauty, by banishing her to her couch, for the couch [the bed] is the place of temptation and enticement, where the rebellious woman reaches the summit of her power. If the man can conquer his disposition against her temptation, then he has disarmed her from her sharpest and most treasured weapon." Another Islamic commentator speaks on the same Surah and states: "This sexual desertion is a remedy that curbs the rebelliousness of the woman, and humiliates her pride, in that which she treasures most, her femininity . . . thus inflicting the most humiliating defeat on the woman."[42]

Chapter Six

Muhammad and His Followers on Free Speech

One of the greatest of blessings enjoyed under the American system is freedom of speech. Conservatives and liberals have access to the media. Those who agree with the government on a particular point, as well as those who don't, can freely voice their views, write articles and books with the result being that the general public is allowed to make their own decisions on a variety of matters.

But it is this openness that makes America and the American way of life an affront to Islam. America represents a dangerous example of the power of secular values to win people's hearts.

With modern technology, America exerts an influence on the Islamic world. Illegal satellite dishes in Muslim dictatorships receive forbidden programs from U.S. television broadcasts. The same technology that engineers such American broadcasts is also used to gain victory against primitive Islamic warriors who claim to have confidence in Allah. One writer stated that "Islam puts God at its center. The Western world, on the other hand, is concerned with liberalism, freedom, and democracy. It's absolute heresy. And worst of all, from the Islamists' point of view, this culture is increasingly successful."[43]

Despite Claims, Islam Cannot Allow Free Speech

While Muslims will claim that Islam allows free speech, they have to redefine the concept. In the tract *Choosing Islam* we read:

> Islam gives the right of freedom of thought and expression to all citizens of the Islamic state on the condition that it should be used for the propagation of virtue and truth and not for spreading evil and wickedness. The Islamic concept of freedom of expression is much superior to the concept prevalent in the West. Under no circumstances would Islam allow evil and wickedness to be propagated. It also does not give anybody the right to use abusive or offensive language in the name of criticism. It was the practice of the Muslims to enquire from the Holy Prophet whether on a certain matter a divine injunction had been revealed to him. If he said that he had received no divine injunction, the Muslims freely expressed their opinion on the matter.

The "free speech" described here is not free speech. "Freedom" means "freedom from restraint." Muslims will counter that even in America there is not absolute freedom of speech. We agree. Even in a free society there must be some restraint, but it is not restraint that is based on the teachings of an official, state-supported religion.

I am not free to shout "fire" in a crowded room. Such an action would cause a rush of people to the exit and many could be killed or injured. However, the prohibition against shouting "fire" under such conditions is not a prohibition that is based on a particular religion, but on other considerations.

In the above quotation, "freedom" and "freedom of expression" are concepts limited by religious dogma as interpreted by the ruling religious elite. This is not "freedom" in the sense that the word is used in America. The reason for the difference is that the U.S. Constitution rejects the concept of an official state religion. The United States was not intended by its founders to become a theocratic kingdom, whereas Islam is seeking to establish a theocracy that is under the rule of the Koran. In an Islamic theocratic state anyone teaching that Jesus Christ is the eternal Son of God is teaching "evil." In the kind of state envisioned under the United States Constitution, however, teaching that Jesus Christ is the eternal Son of God is neither regarded as being good or evil. It is not a matter with which the government should be concerned.

Because of this theocratic orientation, an Islamic state does not and cannot allow free speech, freedom of expression, or religious liberty.

Ali Dashti, an Iranian Muslim scholar, knew this quite well. He was afraid to tell the truth about Islam. In his book, *Twenty-three Years: The Life of the Prophet Mohammed*, he cites numerous grammatical errors in the Koran, so many, in fact, that the rules of grammar had to be changed in order to fit the claim that the Koran is without error. There was one precaution he had to take, however. He stipulated that the book would be published posthumously—after his death.[44] Now why would a scholar stipulate such a thing unless he was convinced that he really didn't enjoy freedom of speech?

Free Speech or Lying Words?

In the tract *Human Rights in Islam*, the author uses the same word-twisting in claiming that Islamic governments give its citizens free speech as was found in the above-cited tract *Choosing Islam*: "Islam gives the right of freedom of thought and expression to all citizens of the Islamic state. . . ." It looks so good, so American, doesn't it?

But the sentence continues with the words ". . . on the condition that it should be used for the propagation of virtue and truth and not for spreading evil and wickedness." Be careful. This is not freedom of thought and expression. The catch is in the words "on the condition that it should be used for the propagation of virtue and truth and not for spreading evil and wickedness." This means, among other things, that the Christian does not have freedom of thought and expression. For the Christian to teach that Jesus Christ is the eternal Son of God would be considered the "spreading of evil and wickedness."

Isn't there something inherently sneaky about a person who will tell you that you have freedom of thought and expression when you really don't?

The author goes on to state that Islam allows the protection of all religious sentiments: "Along with freedom of conviction and freedom of conscience, Islam has given the right to the individual that his religious sentiments will be given due respect and nothing will be said or done which may encroach upon his right." Don't believe it. The last fourteen hundred years of Islamic tyranny in the Middle East and elsewhere clearly proves that this is a lie.

The Sword of Islam? Magic or Death?

In another tract, this one entitled *The Sword of Islam*, we are led to believe that we have been mistaken about this sword. It is not a blade of steel, but a blade of magic:

> The first few who embraced the "new" religion in Makkah in the Arabian Peninsula at the hands of the prophet, were his wife Khadijah, his servant Zaid, and his eleven year old cousin Ali . . . they simply couldn't resist the MAGIC SWORD of a humble and lonely prophet! . . . The Muslim emigrants to Madinah brought their SWORD with them. The SWORD continued to work and it's *(sic)* magnetic force continued to "pull" people towards it until the whole of Arabia joined the Faith. . . . So sharp was the edge of the SWORD! It simply conquered the hearts; bodies yielded automatically. It is the SWORD OF TRUTH, whose mere shine eliminates falsehood just like light wipes away darkness. HAS THE SWORD GONE BLUNT? NO, FAR FROM IT.

I do not doubt that for some the teaching of Islam has a magnetic pull. But, historically, Muslim leaders have not been too confident in magnetism and have resorted to a sharp steel blade.

Islamic Compassion:
No Sword If They Say "I'm Sorry"

When Christian Nigerian reporter Isioma Daniel suggested that Muhammad might have chosen a bride from among the Miss World contestants, violence exploded in Nigeria and Miss Daniel had to flee to America after one of the officials of Nigeria's Zamfara State told a rally that the Muslim faithful should behead her.

However, Nigeria's Supreme Council for Islamic Affairs said the official who made the comment about beheading Miss Daniel had no authority to issue what was essentially a *fatwa*—an official sentence of death. Other Muslim officials agreed and reportedly shared the "compassionate" side of Islam. Sheikh Saadal-Saleh, an official of Saudi Arabia's Ministry of Islamic affairs stated: "They have no right to kill if the person expresses regret."[45] There now, doesn't such compassion make you want to convert?

The hypocrisy of this Saudi official is brazen and bold. He thought he was making Islam look nice. But what if the newspaper did not express regret? What if the newspaper felt that the statement was legitimate? Then would the sentence of death be valid?

Statements like this should warn all Americans, including the president, against trusting the Saudis. That government has launched a massive propaganda campaign within the United States to convince Americans that Saudi Arabia is really a moderate Islamic state that is in full support of America's war on terrorism. Saudi crown prince Abdullah bin Abdulazziz al-Saud has been telling President Bush how much he regrets that a number of young Saudi citizens have been enticed by evil forces to attack America.

The Saudis are clearly seeking to silence the critics. It was recently reported that: "Under fire for its alleged support of terrorism, Saudi Arabia revealed details . . . about its internal campaign to crack down on al-Qaeda and

lashed out at U.S. critics for engaging in a 'feeding fren-
zy' against a long-time ally."[46]

One would hope that the Saudis are sincere in com-
bating terrorism. We, however, have to be on the alert.
Saudi Arabia is based on Islamic law. The most holy book
of Islam, the Koran, states:

Fighting is prescribed for you. . . .

—Surah 2:216

Fight and slay the pagans wherever you find them.
Beleaguer them, and lie in wait for them in every strat-
agem of war. . . .

—Surah 9:5

Fight in the way of Allah . . . and slay them [unbeliev-
ers] wherever you find them and drive them out . . .
and fight them until . . . religion is for Allah. . . .

—Sura 2:190–193

"Freedom of Speech" Under Islam

It is hard to believe that anyone could claim that Islam
allows freedom of expression when there are so many
examples proving the contrary. Though Salman Rushdie
is the best example of how Islam silences those it doesn't
like, there are many other examples.

• *Nasr Hamid Abu Zayd*—An Egyptian professor of literature who wrote that certain references in the Koran
to supernatural events should really be taken meta-
phorically. As a result, his marriage was dissolved by
an Egyptian court on the grounds that his writings
proved him to be a non-Muslim. According to Islamic

law, a Muslim woman cannot be married to a non-Muslim. Abu Zayd's writing qualified him as a non-Muslim, hence the dissolution of his marriage.

• *Farag Foda*—An Egyptian intellectual who scorned radical Islam and was shot to death.

• *Naguib Mahfouz*—This elderly Nobel Prize laureate for literature was seriously injured in Cairo, Egypt, when an attacker stabbed him in the neck.

• *Makin Morcos*—An Egyptian who was murdered in Australia for criticizing the militant Islamic campaign against Christians in his native country.

• *Rashad Khalifa*—An Egyptian biochemist living in Tucson, Arizona, who was stabbed to death in January 1990 to put an end to his so-called heretical ideas.

• *Steven Emerson*—A former Senate aide and investigative reporter for *U.S. News & World Report,* CNN, and other media, received numerous death threats for his award-winning documentary, *Jihad in America.*[47]

Where are the free speech rights of these individuals? Those who say there is freedom of speech under Islam must be labeled for what they are: liars. Revelation 21:8 describes their final doom: ". . . and all liars, shall have their part in the lake which burneth with fire and brimstone. . . ."

As a Christian I can sympathize with Muslim reformers who honestly admit that the Koran has some problems that make it difficult to consistently apply its teachings in today's world. I have a certain degree of admiration for their work and their bold stand. But how have Islamic reformers been treated? Does their treatment verify the claims that Islam allows freedom of expression and thought?

The Fate of Islamic Reform Movements

The Islamic reform movement began in earnest in the 1980s as the secular ideologies that replaced colonialism left hearts yearning for something more lasting. Various forms of nationalism and socialism that followed hard on the heels of colonialism could not fill the emptiness of the human heart. The upheaval of traditional values and the dissemination of new ideas through mass communication led to the development of a reform movement. One of its characteristics is the conviction that Islamic traditions can be understood in a variety of ways and that a pluralism of beliefs is healthy. The Islamic reform movement is seeking to reconcile Islam with modern society by creating a worldview that is compatible with both.

Two Muslim thinkers have spearheaded this movement. Abdul Karim Soroush is a Shi'ite Muslim from Iran. Sheikh Rachid al-Ghannouchi is a Sunni Muslim and a Tunisian Arab. Al-Ghannouchi is the exiled leader of Hezb al-Nahda (Party of the Renaissance), the party that has been trying to create a new Islamic republic in Tunisia. Since the mid-1990s Soroush and al-Ghannouchni have produced influential essays relating to the question of Islam and democracy. Have they been allowed to disseminate their ideas freely?

In Iran, Soroush's ideas have not been well received by the ruling religious elite. In a November 1995 address commemorating the 1979 U.S. embassy takeover, Ayatollah Ali Khamenei spent more time condemning Soroush's views than he did attacking Israel or the United States.

At Tehran University in the autumn of 1995, more than a hundred members of Ansar (Helpers of the Party of God) beat up on Soroush as he tried to give a special address that the Muslim Students' Association had invited him to deliver. Many were injured. The attack then sparked an on-campus demonstration in favor of Soroush. As a result, a new law was passed imposing severe penalties on anyone who espoused ideas critical of Iran's Islamic republic or who even associated with those who espoused such ideas.[48]

There are many other similar episodes that can be cited to challenge the contention that Islam allows anything that even resembles freedom of expression. In fact, the most damaging critique of Islam is the fact that Islamic moderates admit that Islam needs to be moderated. Robin Wright, who argues that Islam is compatible with democracy and who favors Shoroush's views, nevertheless recognizes the totalitarian leanings inherent in Islam.

> Islam is a religion that can still grow, Soroush argues. It should not be used as a modern ideology, for it is too likely to become totalitarian. Yet he believes in *shari'a,* or Islamic law, as a basis for modern legislation. And *shari'a,* too, can grow. "*Shari'a* is something expandable. You cannot imagine the extent of its flexibility," he has said, adding that "in an Islamic democracy, you can actualize all its potential flexibility."[49]

Other Kinds of Intimidation

While Islam has used violence and threats of force to intimidate those who would freely express themselves, Islamists are developing other impediments to the exercise of free speech.

In the U.S. and Canada, for example, they are becoming adept at lobbying techniques, and know how to cry "profiling!" and "racial discrimination!" Those who expose their devices are called writers of "hate literature." Muslims are also learning more about legal maneuvers and the rights they have in Western societies, all for the purpose of elevating Islam in the West to the status that it has in other parts of the world.

In France, an outspoken Catholic Bishop, Marcel Lefebvre, was fined nearly one thousand dollars under French law for stating that when the Muslim presence in France becomes more dominant "it is your wives, your daughters, your children who will be kidnapped and dragged off to a certain kind of place as they exist [in Morocco]." In Canada, a Christian street preacher protesting the persecution of Christians by Muslims was accused by Muslim organizations of "inciting hatred" and found guilty of violating Canada's hate-speech laws. As a consequence he was sentenced to two hundred forty hours of community service. At the U.N., when the topic of slavery in the Sudan or when Muslim anti-Semitism is raised, the words "blasphemy" and "the defamation of Islam" are shouted out and shut off the possibility of the intelligent discussion of these important issues.[50]

In addition, Muslims are also taking legal action in Canada against high-profile Christians. In a report filed by Art Moore and appearing in *WorldNetDaily.com* (November 14, 2002) we read that a leading Islamic group in Canada is preparing to take legal action under Canada's hate-crimes laws against the broadcast of Rev. Jerry Falwell, who asserted that "Muhammad is a terrorist."

The Canadian law prohibits any public statement that "willfully promotes hatred" against various groups. Taken at face value, the law bears a certain degree of validity. However, the law can readily be interpreted to ban the public presentation of various religious views. It is the nature of religious statements—whether in the Bible, the Koran, the Talmud or a host of other writings dealing with God, ethics, and values—to warn adherents of that religion against certain groups and behaviors. The Canadian Islamic Congress, the group preparing to take legal action against Mr. Falwell, could easily be cited for violations of the law because of the writings and actions of its leading Prophet, Muhammad.

Semantic Smog

Muslims sometimes respond to the charge of censorship by claiming that the West practices its own brand of censorship and is therefore hypocritical in speaking about Isalmic censorship. One of the proponents of this charge, Ali A. Marzui, writes:

> Many devout Muslims felt that Rushdie had no right to poke fun at and twist into obscenity some of the most sacred symbols of Islam. Most Muslim countries banned the novel because officials there considered it morally repugnant. Western intellectuals argued that as an artist, Rushdie had the sacred right and even duty to go wherever his imagination led him in his writing. Yet until the 1960s, *Lady Chatterley's Lover* [a novel by D. H. Lawrence] was regarded as morally repugnant under British law for daring to depict an affair between a married member of the gentry and a worker on the estate. For a long time after Oscar Wilde's conviction for homosexual acts, *The Picture of Darwin Gray* was regarded as morally repugnant. Today other gay writers are up against a wall of prejudice.[51]

This is a smokescreen, deliberately blown across our paths to cloud the issues. We are not just talking about banning Rushdie's works—Muslims are free to do that—but about *death threats and violence*.

Ayatollah Khomeini, the revolutionary ruler of Iran, who took prompt and drastic action: On February 14, 1989, he called upon "all zealous Muslims quickly to execute" not just Salman Rushdie as the author of *The Satanic Verses* but "all those involved in its publication who were aware of its content." This edict led to emergency measures in England to protect Rushdie's person, and to weeks and months of intense debate among the world' politicians and intellectuals about the issues of freedom of speech and blasphemy.[52]

Turn Over the Rushdies of the World to the Islamic Butchers?

In an essay entitled "U.S. Policies Incite Islamic Terrorism," Haroon Siddiqui argues that the West has created a climate in which Islamic terrorism flourishes. One of the reasons he gives: "The West's harboring of those who poke fun at Islam (especially Salman Rushdie, author of *Satanic Verses*)."[53] According to this, the West is to blame for Islamic terrorism because we allow freedom of speech. Does that tell you what would happen if America became an Islamic nation?

Siddiqui also fault's America's foreign policy which is "heavily pro-Israeli."[54] Just as he wants America to turn dissidents like Rushdie over to Islamic fanatics, he evidently wants America to abandon her only true ally in the Middle East to Islamic fanatics. "The Home of the

Brave and the Land of the Free" should now please terrorists by refusing to shelter those who are being attacked by terrorists. We will then become "the Home of the Cowardly and the Land of the Fearful."

Israelis have been subjected to one atrocity after another by Islamic fanatics. Following a recent attack by Palestinian suicide bombers, Secretary of State Colin Powell pleaded with the Palestinians to issue some form of denunciation of the crimes. Arafat complained that only the Palestinian side is ever required to denounce terrorism. A Jewish research scientist in Tel Aviv, whose identity I will not reveal, comments on this.

Perhaps the Palestinians have a point, and so to set the record straight, I do hereby denounce the following in the name of the Jewish people:

1. All Jewish suicide bombers who have ever acted against Arabs.

2. All Arab buses blown up by Jews.

3. All Arab pizza parlors, malls, discotheques, and restaurants destroyed by Jewish terrorists.

4. All airplanes hijacked by Jews since 1903.

5. All Ramadan feasts targeted by Jewish suicide bombers.

6. All Arabs lynched in Israeli cities; all Arab Olympic athletes murdered by Jews; all Arab embassies bombed by Jews.

7. All Jewish school books which claim that Arabs poison wells, use Christian blood to bake pita, control world finance, and murdered Jesus; and that Arab elders meet secretly to plot a world takeover.

8. And I am particularly ashamed at the way my fellow Jews attacked the World Trade Center, Penta-

gon, and civilian aircraft on September 11, and then danced in the streets to celebrate the act.

The Devious Work of American Liberals

Muslims overseas are not the only ones blaming America for Islamic terrorism against America. Oubai Shahbandar is an Arab student at Arizona State. He has met the most vicious animosity imaginable, both from the student body and the university's administration. Why? Because of his pro-American stance. In a recent *WorldNet-Daily* report Shahbandar writes:

> It all began last year when, immediately following the terror attacks of 9-11, a slew of "teach ins" were held—sponsored in part by university funds—imploring fellow ASU students to "understand the reasoning behind 9-11." This, in turn, became a series of hour-long sessions dedicated to "educating" the students on how "imperialism" and America's lack of concern for "international social justice" led to the horrific attacks. In essence, we were being sold the seditious lie that it was "America's fault," that the terrorists were merely reacting to far greater atrocities on our part. Never mind the fact that countless Arab and Muslim families like mine found refuge in the freedom and prosperity that this great nation bestowed upon them. Never mind the fact that no other country on earth could provide my family the same luxuries and liberties that they enjoy now as American citizens.
>
> I, as most people do, see this nation of ours as being fundamentally good and generous to those that have come to seek refuge from the tyranny and oppression plaguing the majority of humanity. The fact

that my university was actively sponsoring an educational environment where that very goodness was being vilified and defamed, frankly, revolted and enraged me.[55]

Chapter Seven

Muhammad and His Followers on the Authority of Scripture

Many of the claims made by Muslims concern the accuracy and reliability of the Christian Scriptures. In several places the Koran teaches respect for the Old and New Testaments, but then in other places, it suggests that the Old and New Testaments have been corrupted. This means that if we want to know the truth, according to the Muslim, we have to get it from the Koran, not from the Bible.

Evaluating the Claims

Both the Bible and the Koran claim to come from God. What would Muslims need to support their claim that the Bible has been corrupted?

1. Examples of the corruption of the Scripture by showing original and ancient manuscripts that support the

Koran and therefore supply factual documentary evidence that corruption has indeed taken place.

2. Reasons why Jews and Christians would want to change the Scripture. It is hard to believe that Jews and Christians would want to change the Word of God. Some of the harshest statements in the Bible are directed against those who would add to, or subtract from, the Scripture. The idea of changing Scripture to support some personal agenda (against Muhammad or anyone else) is abhorrent to both Jews and Christians.

3. Different editions of the Bible. The controversy would be decided in favor of Islam if there was proof that the Bible of Muhammad's day was different than the Bible of the first century A.D., or, if there was proof that the Bible in the centuries following Muhammad's day is different than the Bible of the first century A.D.

The Koran and the Bible

While it is clear that the Bible does not support the Koran and Muslim theology based on it, what is not well known is the fact that there are several statements in the Koran that are supportive of the Bible.

Significantly, the Koran presents a Jesus that is far more noble than Muhammad! The Jesus of the Koran was virgin born and spoke as an infant—something that Muhammad did not do (Surah 19:20–22,29–33). The Koran also teaches that Jesus was taken up to Allah and that he will be a witness against the unbelievers on the day of resurrection (Surah 4:157,159). Amazingly, when the Christian reads the Koran he finds an extra-biblical source indicating that Jesus is the Messiah!

Another surprise is that Surah 10:94 encourages the

Prophet Muhammad to listen to the people of the Book—
Jews and Christians. This verse of the Koran is so far-
reaching that Islamic scholars have to add bracketed words
of explanation to make it suit Islamic readers. In the *Translation of the Meaning of the Noble Qur'an in the English
Language,* with translation and explanatory notes by two
Saudi scholars, Dr. Muhammad Taqi-ud-Din al-Hilali and
Dr. Muhammad Muhsin Khan, the meaning of Surah
10:94 is given as follows:

> So, if you (O Muhammad) are in doubt concerning
> that which we have revealed unto you, [i.e., that your
> name is written in the Taurat (Torah) and the Injeel
> (Gospel)], then ask those who are reading the Book
> [the Taurat (Torah) and the Injeel (Gospel)] before
> you. Verily, the truth has come to you from your Lord.
> So be not of those who doubt (it).[56]

We notice that the two Saudi scholars have inserted some
words in brackets that are not in the text of the Koran,
namely the words "that your name is written in the Tau-
rat (Torah) and the Injeel (Gospel)." One can readily see
why these words were added. The koranic text without
the bracketed words is an embarrassment. Without the
added words, the koranic text states: "O Muhammad, if
you are in doubt concerning what we have revealed to
you, then ask those who read the Bible, namely Christians and Jews."

Concerning this embarrassing Surah, former Muslims
Ergun and Emir Caner write: "Here Muhammad places
the veracity of his words on par with the authenticity of
the Bible as it was available in the seventh century." They
proceed to point out that since "the Bible of the seventh
century is the Bible of today, any contention that the Bi-

ble is corrupt opposes the words of Muhammad, who represented the final revelation of Allah to the world. Surely Muhammad would not have asked his followers to accept a corrupted version of the New Testament."[57]

There are several other statements in the Koran that reflect a high view of the Christian Bible, as the following verses from the Koran reveal:

• Surah 3:2-3: "There is no god but Him, the Living, the Ever-existent One. He has revealed to you the Book with the Truth, confirming the scriptures which preceded it; for He has already revealed the Torah and the Gospel for the guidance of mankind, and the distinction between right and wrong."

  Comment: Allah, according to this Surah, has confirmed the scriptures which preceded the Koran. The Torah (Old Testament law) and the Gospel have been given by Allah and are the Word of God. Since God's Word cannot change and since the Scriptures of the seventh century and the earlier centuries are the same as the Hebrew-Christian Scriptures of today, they are indeed, according to the Koran, the Word of God.

• Surah 4:136: "Believers, have faith in God and His apostle, in the Book He has revealed to His apostle, and in the Scriptures He formerly revealed. He that denies God, His angels, His Scriptures, His apostles, and the Last Day has gone far astray."

  Comment: Muslims are encouraged to trust in "the Scriptures He formerly revealed." The Christian Scriptures were revealed before Muhammad received the Koran.

• Surah 5:44–48: "We have revealed the Torah, in which there is guidance and light. By it the prophets who

surrendered themselves judged the Jews, and so did
the rabbis and the divines, according to God's Book
which had been committed to their keeping and to
which they themselves were witnesses. . . . After them
We sent forth Jesus, the son of Mary, confirming the
Torah already revealed, and gave him the Gospel, in
which there is guidance and light, corroborating what
was revealed before it in the Torah, a guide and an
admonition to the righteous. Therefore let those who
follow the Gospel judge according to what God has
revealed therein. . . . And to you We have revealed
the Book with the truth. It confirms the Scriptures
which came before it and stands as a guardian over
them."

Comment: The Torah has been revealed to mankind and was committed to "the rabbis and the divines." Since Muslims have not been able to offer any
proof that the "Torah" as we have it today has been
corrupted, we must conclude that the Koran has a
high view of the Bible.

♦ Surah 10:37: "This Koran could not have been de-
vised by any but God. It confirms what was revealed
before it and fully explains the Scriptures. It is beyond doubt from the Lord of the universe."

Comment: The Koran, which this Surah states is of
Divine origin, "fully explains" the Bible. On the basis
of this if the Koran is of Divine origin, so is the Bible.
An honest Muslim seeker, therefore, will read the Bible with an open mind. The Koran requires it.

Has the Bible Been Corrupted?

There are many standard works demonstrating that the
Bible has not been corrupted. Rather than just covering

old ground, we will answer this question as it pertains, in particular, to the challenges of Muslim writers.

We can say, without any fear of contradiction, that the Bible that we have today is basically the same Bible as was available thousands of years ago. There has never been a Bible that taught Islamic doctrine. Muslims are at a loss to empirically back up their contention that the Bible as we have it today teaches different doctrines than the "original" Bible.

What kind of empirical proof would be needed by Muslim apologists? Ancient manuscripts showing that the early church believed in an Islamic Jesus, or ancient manuscripts differing doctrinally from the New Testament of today. Even the inferior Westcott-Hort text of modern translations does not teach an Islamic Jesus, nor does it even suggest that the Koran is "the Word of God." While we believe that there are serious omissions from the Westcott-Hort text, Christian apologists who write against Islam often use the newer translations in their arguments.

There are literally thousands of ancient New Testament manuscripts that prove beyond a shadow of a doubt that there never has been an "Islamic New Testament" that was later corrupted by Christians and Jews. In addition to these manuscripts, there are thousands of quotations of the New Testament by the early church fathers. These early Christians so completely quoted the New Testament in their sermons and theological writings that we could reconstruct almost all of the New Testament just from these ancient quotations. A careful compilation of the data shows that the early Christians quoted all of the New Testament with the exception of eleven verses. There are more than thirty-six thousand quotations of the New Testament from just seven of the church fathers.[58]

The Question of Biblical Variants

Muslims, along with liberals and others who try to undermine the Bible, often make much of the variants found in the early manuscripts, especially in the New Testament. They will say that there are over two hundred thousand variants in the New Testament alone, and by this observation will conclude that the New Testament has been so hopelessly corrupted that no one can possibly ever know what the originals were like.

And now for the rest of the story . . .

While it is true that there are over two hundred thousand variants, they are all inconsequential. Many of those are variants in spelling, grammar, or word order. None of the variants change any doctrine of the Christian faith such as: the necessity of the new birth, the deity of Jesus Christ, the trinitarian nature of God, salvation by the grace of God through faith in Christ alone, the substitutionary death of Christ and His vicarious atonement, plus many others. We will illustrate the nature of the variants by looking at the following statements.

Text: "For God so loved the world that he gave his only begotten Son."

Variant #1: "For God loved the world so much that he gave his only begotten Son."

Variant #2: "For Gd so loved the world that he gave his only begotten Son."

Variant #3: "Indeed God so loved the whole world that he gave his only begotten Son."

None of these variants change the meaning and theology of the text. We do not find variants in the manuscripts that state: "God does not love the world, therefore he gave his only begotten Son," or, "God so loved the world that he gave his daughter. . . ." And there are no variants that ever endorse Muslim theology.

Christians have no problems with the variants in the ancient manuscripts, just as they have no problem with the Four Gospels and the fact that they sometimes give slightly different, but complementary, accounts of the same incident. That they exist is proof that there was no conspiracy to alter the message. If there had been such a conspiracy, there would have been great uniformity. The textual history of the Bible argues that it is free from corruption.

Despite the denials of Muslim apologists, the Koran also has a textual history. The Koran did not just drop out of the sky in its present form, nor was an original edition found out in the desert somewhere.

When Caliph Uthman discovered the many variants in the Koran, he collected all the copies and had them all burned—except one codex which he felt was the "right one." This became the official text of the Koran. In comparing the textual history of the Bible with the Koran, Christian apologist Winfried Corduan comments that "the very existence of so many variant readings allows us to recover what the original must have said with a great degree of confidence. By contrast, it is impossible to restore the Quran to what existed prior to Uthman, since we now have only one version of the Quran—the one Uthman wanted us to have."[59]

The Bible and Prophecy

The fulfillment of biblical prophecy is concrete proof that the Bible is indeed the very Word of God. We can check these prophecies because

many of them *have already* been fulfilled—and they have been fulfilled exactly as predicted by the ancient prophets.

Let's look, for example, at the ancient prophecies concerning the first coming of Jesus Christ. Many of them are of such a nature that they could not have been deliberately fulfilled by a fake. It is impossible for a person to have "staged" the place and manner of His birth, His life, and the method of His execution a thousand years before it even happened! Noteworthy is Psalm 22 which describes Jesus' death by crucifixion ten centuries before crucifixion became a method of execution.

Fulfilled Prophecies Regarding Jesus Christ

Prophecy	Topic	Fulfillment
Gen. 12:12	Seed of Abraham	Matt. 1:1; Gal. 3:16
Gen. 49:10	From Judah	Matt. 1:2
2 Sam. 7:12–16	Descendant of David	Matt. 1:1
Isaiah 7:14	Virgin Conception	Matt. 1:23
Micah 5:2	Born in Bethlehem	Matt. 2:6
Isa. 40:3; Mic. 3:1	John, forerunner	Matt. 3:3
Numb. 24:17; Ps. 2:6	King	Matt. 21:5
Deut. 18:15–18	Prophet	Acts 3:22–23
Ps. 110:4	Priest	Heb. 5:6–10
Ps. 22:1	Sin-bearer	Matt. 27:46
Ps. 22:7–8	Mocked	Matt. 27:39,43
Ps. 22:16	Hands, feet pierced	Jn. 20:25
Ps. 22:17	No bones broken	Jn. 19:33–36
Ps. 22:18	Soldiers gambled	Jn. 19:24
Isa. 52:14	Disfigured	Jn. 19:1
Isa. 53:5	Scourging and death	Jn. 19:1,18
Ps. 16:10; 22:22	Resurrection	Matt. 28:6; Acts 2:27–28
Ps. 68:18	Ascension	Lk. 24:50; Acts 1:9–11

Daniel's "Weeks of Years"

Muslims claim that the Bible has been tampered with and

the true Word of God has been corrupted in a conspiracy against Islam. However, the Bible was completed hundreds of years before the birth of Muhammad in A.D. 570. How could the Word of God have been changed to undermine the truth of Islam when Islam had not even come into existence? This is like saying that the United States Constitution was intentionally worded to contradict and undermine the U.N. Charter. But the Constitution of the United States was written many years before there was even a U.N. Charter. It would be far more reasonable to claim that the U.N. Charter was deliberately worded to contradict and undermine the U.S. Constitution.

We can show that the claim that the Scriptures were corrupted is false by comparing an important biblical prophecy with ancient history.

Daniel's prophecy of the seventy weeks (Dan. 9:24–27) reveals the exact scheduling of future events before they even happened. In 539 B.C. (Dan. 9:1–2) a messenger from God came to Daniel with the prophecy of the seventy weeks. Daniel 9:25 reveals that a four hundred ninety-year period of time has been ordained by God for the Jewish people to accomplish several things. Daniel 9:25–26 states: "Know therefore and understand, that from the going forth of the commandment to restore and to build Jerusalem unto the Messiah the Prince shall be seven weeks [seven sevens=forty-nine years], and three score and two weeks [sixty-two sevens (434 years), totaling sixty-nine sevens=483 years]: the street shall be built again, and the wall, even in troublous times. And after threescore and two weeks shall Messiah be cut off, but not for himself. . . ."

Counting four hundred eighty-three years forward from the issuing of the commandment, or decree, "to restore and build Jerusalem," which scholars agree was the decree of King Artaxerxes (Neh. 2:1–10) which was issued in the spring of 444 B.C. we find an amazing correspondence with what actually happened—yet it was prophesied more than one hundred years before the event!

The ancient Hebrew year consisted of three hundred sixty days (twelve months of thirty days each). By multiplying 360 days times 483 years we come out with 173,880 days, which would place the crucifixion of Christ—the cutting off of Messiah but not for Himself—in the spring of A.D. 33.

Daniel the Prophet

The prophecies of Daniel are so uncannily accurate that liberal scholars have often claimed that though the book of Daniel claims to be a prophecy, it is really a history. In other words, Daniel is not predicting what will happen, but he is simply recounting what has already happened. Rather than being a prophet, Daniel is a careful historian. The enemies of the Bible like to make this claim about Daniel 11. That chapter speaks about the intrigues and battles of the Seleucids and Ptolemies (descendants of the generals of Alexander the Great) so minutely and with such precision that Daniel could not possibly (so the enemies of Scripture claim) have predicted these things. This must be history, or so they say.

However, there can be no reasonable doubt that the book of Daniel is really a prophecy and that it was written in the sixth century B.C. The mention of Belshazzar (Dan. 5), for example, was not an historical error. This has been verified from the historical Nabonidus Chronicle. Not only do the international contracts of the Neo-Babylonian Empire account for the presence of foreign words in the book, but recent linguistic research proves false the arguments for the alleged lateness of the book of Daniel. Furthermore, sections of the book have been found in the Dead Sea Scrolls which date from about 200 B.C. The book of Daniel is not history. It is prophetic. The information in Daniel could not have been altered later by the Gospel writers so that it would "match" the time of the death of Christ.

With modern archaeology, detailed chronologies, and consistent methods of dating, we are now able to determine the dates of Old Testament events with greater ease and accuracy than ever before. While the chronologists of the Old Testament kept careful records—something that has been verified over and over again—the Gospel writers were fishermen, not scribal chronologists. They could not have known precisely how much time had passed since the issuing of the decree referred to in Daniel 9 and Nehemiah 2.

For the human authors of the Gospel accounts to have deliberately contrived the date of the death of Christ and to fit it in with the prophecy of the first sixty-nine weeks of Daniel's seventy weeks would require that they would have to know the precise date they were faking and also the specific criteria modern scholars would use to fix the date! It is irrational to claim that the accuracy of the date given was a deliberate lie because the writers would not have been able to lie with such precision!

Verification from Later Secular Sources

We know from ancient secular sources, Josephus and the Roman historian Tacitus, that there was a religious leader named Jesus, who was known as "the founder of the Christian sect," who was crucified under the authority of

Pontius Pilate in Judea.

What these secular sources record about Jesus matches quite well with the information we have recorded in the New Testament. By the middle of the first century the Christian movement was gaining converts in large numbers, which points to the existence of a founder (Jesus Christ) some years earlier (around A.D. 30). We can fix the date with even more precision when we realize that Pilate would have only been in that position of authority to execute Jesus during that same period of time. With all of this information, no serious historian who gives any degree of credence to the ancient documents doubts the existence of the One whom we call "Jesus."

Do we really believe that Judeo-Christian conspirators tampered with the Word of God? If we are tempted to do so, we need to remember that these amazing prophecies were written hundreds of years before Jesus Christ came on the scene. Many of the details of the prophecies were not under the control of the individual being prophesied about. For Jesus to have arranged the details of His death was far out of the scope of human ability because an ordinary person would have no way to enlist the cooperation of the Roman and Jewish authorities whose actions had been prophesied by God centuries before.

Chapter Eight

A Clear
and Present Danger[60]

I believe I have presented enough proof to alert the reader that unwarranted claims are being made by Muslim apologists for the purpose of deceiving the American public. All that glitters is not gold, and all that we are being told about Islam is not true. It's hard for me to believe that the purveyors of these lies do not know their own history and that what they are writing they are writing in ignorance.

The ancient Gibeonites delivered themselves from doom through deception. It was a clever plan that worked. They fooled the Israelite soldiers by acting as if they had come from a great distance. Though the Israelites tried to substantiate their story by examining their dry and moldy bread, their worn out shoes, and their tattered garments, they neglected the most important test—they "asked not counsel at the mouth of the Lord" (Josh. 9:14).

Christians will never have a clear picture of what is

happening in our world apart from a knowledge of the Scripture, biblical prophecy, and the extent of the spiritual warfare being waged all around us.

The Ignorance Is Pervasive

On a recent trip to a coastal resort city in the southern U.S. I met a man whom we will call Moshe [not his real name]. Moshe had a mechanical right arm—from his shoulder down. My buddy and I began to speak to him and found that he was an Israeli who had served with the Israeli Defense Forces. About a year prior to our meeting him, Moshe and his buddies in the military were on a bus in Jerusalem. A Palestinian suicide bomber got on the bus. The bomber blew himself up and killed several of the Israeli soldiers. Moshe's right arm was removed by the force of the blast. As could be imagined, Moshe was bitter.

I made the comment to Moshe that we must love the Palestinian people, as well as all people everywhere because God loves them. I added, however, that we must hate false religions like historical Islam that motivate people to acts of insanity in the name of a false deity.

Moshe quickly interrupted me and said that I had it all wrong. He insisted that the Palestinian people were evil troublemakers, but that Islam is a religion of peace. He did not want to hear anything about God's love for the Palestinians, or that Jesus Christ had shed His blood on Calvary's Cross that they might be saved and spend eternity in heaven.

Red Herring Arguments

Several books have been published since September 11, including my *Religion of Peace or Refuge for Terror?* that prove that Moshe had it backward. He even resorted to the "red herring" argument that Christianity has had its inquisitions and blood purges.

What is a "red herring" argument? In earlier times, when the bloodhounds were closing in, a wise fugitive would drag a smelly red herring across his trail to confuse the dogs. If you speak to someone about Islam today and they don't like what you are saying about that religion, they will drag out the proverbial red herring and attack Christianity. Muslim apologists and politically-correct media reporters have a standard mantra that goes something like: "Well, just look at the Crusades. You Christians have your own terrorists in your past."

Morey's answer to fishy thinking like this is: "It is logically erroneous to set up a parallel between Muslims killing people in *obedience* to the Qur'an and Christians killing people in *disobedience* to the Bible. While the Qur'an commands *jihad,* the New Testament forbids it."[61]

The Hate-Crimes Blame Game

Steve Emerson has done the population of Planet Earth tremendous service with his video *Jihad in America,* which was broadcast on PBS on November 21, 1994. In a recent article, Emerson describes one of the meetings he attended as he was researching the production: "At times spontaneous shouts of 'Kill the Jews' and 'Destroy the West' could be distinctly heard. I had heard such declamatory speakers many times in the Middle East, but it was astonishing to hear it all being preached here in a Middle American capital such as Oklahoma City."[62]

Muslim rights groups, however, protested Emerson's video and were quick to label him as an instigator of hate crimes. "Several weeks before the showing," writes Emerson, "the Council on American-Islamic Relations (CAIR) issued a press release that a mosque in Brooklyn had been set on fire. The subtext: 'PBS "Jihad in America" documentary may prompt more hate crimes.' The implication, of course, was that the violent backlash against Muslims— even a month before the film was to air—had already begun." The fire, however, was not set by anti-Muslim hate groups. "When police investigated the fire," writes Emerson, "they found that it had been set on a rug in an upstairs apartment—over an internal dispute."[63]

The Profiling Blame Game

The airline industry is struggling under serious financial difficulties as a result of the September 11 attacks. The airlines have had the added expense of additional security personnel and equipment, plus the fact that many people are simply afraid to fly. With the fanatic Islamic and Middle Eastern background of the September 11 terrorists, flight crews and pilots are justifiably concerned about Muslim and Middle Eastern travelers. Yet to add insult to injury, Arab-American rights groups are suing the airlines.

In a column appearing in *Arab-American Business* (July 2002) entitled "Rights groups hit airlines with post-Sept. 11 suits; allege profiling and discrimination of Arab-Americans and Muslims," we read: "The suits asked the court to find that the airlines violated the plaintiffs' civil rights and for the airlines to implement measures to prevent future discrimination" (p. 7). Like wolves looking for weak or crippled prey, these groups close in on an ailing industry hoping for a kill. This is not about the rights of minorities but about the destruction of the American economy.

Activists have found that the blame game works well on Americans, many of whom have been made to feel that they are responsible for September 11 and who are apologetic for feeling any anger against the religion and the religious fanatics who brought September 11 on the world. According to nationally-renowned columnist John Leo, Americans aren't mad about September 11 when they should be. This means

> that to avoid anger and judgment, a normal emotional response was diverted into an orgy of self-examination, much of it revolving around the notion that the United States somehow invited or deserved the attacks. The strange reluctance of the National Education Association to identify the attackers (hint: radical Muslim extremists did it) is one expression of how the non-judgmental ethic is applied to 9/11. Linguistic evasion is another: the "tragic events of 9/11" instead of "the terrorist attacks," as if the slaughter was a natural disaster. Of course, everyone knows what happened and who did it, but saying so somehow seems too harsh and judgmental.[64]

While many believe that profiling terrorists is a good idea, they are afraid to admit it. However, profiling is one of the tools of police work and it is sometimes very effective. In a *NewsMax* report (September 10, 2002) entitled "Racial Profiling Saves 189 from al-Qaeda Hijack Attempt," we read that the crew of a London-bound Ryanair Airlines flight in Stockholm used profiling to zero in on a group of Muslim passengers after one of their group had been caught carrying a loaded gun. Though few like to face the facts, the arguments for profiling are compelling. Krauthammer explains by observing that "the pool of suicide bombers is not large. To pretend that it is universal is absurd."[65]

Nevertheless, a don't-hurt-my-feelings paranoia has led security agencies to deny the obvious. "Random passenger checks at airports are completely useless. We've all been there in the waiting lounge, rolling our eyes in disbelief as the eighty-year-old Irish nun, the Hispanic mother of two, the Japanese-American businessman, the House committee chairman with the titanium hip are randomly chosen and subjected to head-to-toe searching for . . . what? Not for security—these people are hardly candidates for suicide terrorism—but for political correctness."[66]

Muslim Immigration

Land of the Free

Recent data shows that Middle Easterners are one of the fastest-growing immigrant groups coming to America. The Center of Immigration Studies indicated that while overall legal and illegal immigration has tripled since 1970, immigration from the Middle East has grown sevenfold.[67]

All of this means one thing: political empowerment. The Arab-American community in Dearborn, Michigan, held its seventh annual Dearborn Arab International Festival. Arab-Americans were quick to note who attended. The editor of an Arab-American publication ecstatically noted: "Politicians showed up to curry favor with the community, the Federal Bureau of Investigation was welcomed by festival organizers, and a large corporate presence was evident. In short, what was clear was that many of the goals the national [Arab-American] community is trying to achieve have, to some degree or another, been realized in the Detroit-Dearborn area. Political empowerment, which for so long has been a cherished goal on the national level, is a reality in Michigan."[68]

Here it is openly admitted that "political empowerment" is the "cherished goal." Will there be religious liberty and freedom for all if a practicing Muslim becomes president? Cal Thomas, writing for the Tribune Media Services (November 2001), answers this with a question: "Is there a country controlled by Islamic militants that guarantees equal rights for all?"

War by Immigration

Almost all of us are immigrants, or come from immigrant families. I love our immigrants and have nothing against *legal* immigration. America has been richly blessed culturally, scientifically, and in every other way by our immigrants who have come to our shores to seek a better life and who have come here to be a part of American society. I have major objections, however, to immigrants who come here to *change* America. This is exactly the intention of large numbers of immigrants from Muslim lands.

Particularly offensive is the tactic of exploiting American freedoms to establish an Islamic society in which there is no freedom. Daniel Pipes, director of the Middle East Forum, and Khalid Duran, state: "Islamists arrive in the United States despising the country and all it represents, intending to make converts, exploit the freedoms and rights granted them, and build a movement that will effect basic changes in the country way of life and its government. . . . Islamists do not accept the United States as it is but want to change it into a majority Muslim country where the Quran replaces the Constitution." They also criticize organizations that claim to represent Muslim political interests, such as the American Muslim Council, the Muslim Public Affairs Committee, and the Council on American-Isalmic Relations (CAIR). "It is striking to note," they write, "that all three organizations are Islamist, and so seek to forward goals deeply at variance with mainstream American principles, as well as the aspirations and concerns of a majority in the Muslim community."[69]

The Goal: An Islamic Takeover

The London-based Arabic newspaper *Al-Hayat* published a series of articles about Muslim communities in Great Britain.[70] One of the individuals interviewed was Sheikh Abu Hamza. Originally from Egypt, Abu Hamza is currently the imam of the Finsbury Park Mosque. Another individual who supplied his insights on the subject was Sheikh Omar Bakri of Syria, currently the founder and head of the Islamic religious court in London. Together they had one message: Christian Europe had better learn to adapt to Islam.

To the question: "Do you identify yourself as British?" Abu Hamza stated: "I see myself as British in the sense that I use my British documents in order to travel. If you mean do I feel British or agree with British politics, then of course, the answer is no. I live here and have a passport. It is a superficial identity. The true identity lies in the heart and spirit. . . . This identity is Islam."

Al-Hayat also asked: "And where does this life, lived in exile, as far as Islam is concerned, lead?" Bakri answered:

> Life for Moslems in exile will bring change in the countries where we live, just as Moslems changed the situation in Abyssinia and Indonesia. With the help of Allah, we will make the west into *Dar al-Islam* [a region

under Islamic rule]. If it is not accomplished from out-side, through invasion of the West by an Islamic state, we will be its army and soldiers from the inside. We will wage an ideological attack without war and kill-ing. Either we will preach to them and they will ac-cept Islam as a spiritual solution for their problems, or we will live among them and they will be influenced by our lifestyle and finally accept Islam.

God's Word has a word for arrogant boasters: "Why do the heathen rage? . . . He that sitteth in the heavens shall laugh: The Lord shall have them in derision" (Ps. 2:1–4). There shall be no hiding place, nor fortification, that will frustrate  Divine judgment. "The pride of thine heart hath deceived thee, thou that dwellest in the clefts of the rock, whose habitation is high; that saith in his heart, Who shall bring me down to the ground? Though thou exalt thyself as the eagle, and though thou set thy nest among the stars, thence will I bring thee down, saith the LORD" (Obad. 3–4).

Chapter Nine
The Mideast Aflame

If we could travel from the sandy wastes of Egypt, north to Israel, and then northeast to Syria, and east to Iraq and Iran, we would be covering some of the most significant territory from the perspective of end-time events. All of these areas are mentioned in biblical prophecy, and all play important roles in relationship to the cataclysmic upheavals of the end times.

Babylon/Iraq

Under the leadership of Saddam Hussein, one of the world's most legendary regions has risen into a position of world prominence. But Babylon, the ancient name for modern Iraq, is not simply legendary in the sense that it appears in legends and fairy tales of good things happening to simple people. It is legendary because it is associated with evil and with all that opposes God.

It was 1980, just one year after Saddam Hussein had ascended to his position of leadership, that Iraq invaded Iran. Though both Iraq and Iran are Muslim nations, the

Iranians do not speak Arabic, but instead they speak Farsi and are Persian rather than Arab. Moreover, there has been centuries of animosity between the two nations. King Hammurabi of Babylon invaded Persia almost eighteen hundred years before Christ. The Persians returned the favor when King Cyrus, king of Persia, conquered Babylon in 539 B.C.

It is hard for many Americans to grasp, but grudges last long in the Middle East. Muslims still speak about what "Christians" did to them in the Crusades ten centuries ago. The feud between the Iraqis (Babylonians) and Iranians (Persians) still simmers as well.

When Saddam invaded Iran in 1980, the Iraqi leader was confident of an easy victory. The Shah had been ousted and Iran and its army was greatly demoralized. But the war that was supposed to end quickly drew on for weeks, months, and then years. In the period from 1982 to 1988, Iraq suffered several humiliating defeats. Baghdad was within range of Iranian missiles. Iraq was not able to sell its oil since its pumping and shipping facilities had been devastated by Iranian shells and bombs. Resentment rose against Saddam. Several assassination attempts were made on his life, but he survived. Something had to be done to pull the people of Iraq together and to give them the assurance that they had a bright and glorious future.

What could Saddam do to encourage the Iraqis on to victory? Would he be able to tap into their ancient heritage to give them a sense of identity with the past? Surely, as far as conquest, empire-building, and the charisma to lead, Nebuchadnezzar might be an example. But did he leave a mandate for his successors?

According to Paul Lewis, as reported in an article entitled "Nebuchadnezzar's Revenge: Iraq Flexes Its Muscles by Rebuilding Babylon," which appeared in the *San Francisco Chronicle* (April 30, 1989), Saddam is operating on the basis of this mandate:

> When King Nebuchadnezzar ran things around here some 2,500 years ago, he left clear instructions for the future kings of Babylon that are finally being carried out. Writing in cuneiform script on tablets of clay, the royal scribes urged their master's successors to repair and rebuild his temples and palaces. Today, in a gesture rich in political significance, President Saddam Hussein, Iraq's strong-armed ruler, is sparing no effort to obey that now-distant command.

We know that though King Nebuchadnezzar made many proud boasts twenty-five hundred years ago, he had not even a small percentage of the military power and kill potential available to Saddam Hussein. And Saddam's weapons could be some of the most ghoulish and destructive imaginable. Though North Korea has been rattling its sabers, the Bush administration has characteristically and consistently regarded Saddam as a greater evil because he has already used some of those weapons on his neighbors.

In his "State of the Union Address," January 29, 2002, President George W. Bush made some direct comments about Saddam Hussein and stated: "He is a dangerous man possessing the world's most dangerous weapons. It is incumbent upon freedom-loving nations to hold him accountable, which is precisely what the United States of America will do."

Several months later, British prime minister Tony Blair wrote his foreword to the British Government Dossier on

Iraq, dated September 24, 2002, and stated: "Saddam has used chemical weapons, not only against an enemy state, but against his own people. Intelligence reports make clear that he sees the building up of his WMD [weapons of mass destruction] capability, as vital to his strategic interests, and in particular his goal of regional domination."

With his grandiose ambitions, Saddam has created fear in the hearts of his neighbors. On June 7, 1981, Israeli warplanes made a dramatic raid on the Osirak nuclear reactor, just outside Baghdad, destroying Iraq's fledgling attempt to develop a nuclear arsenal. At that time I was attending seminary in Fort Worth, Texas. Israel's F-16s were being made at a plant in Fort Worth. We wondered if there would be any retaliation.

No doubt, despite the televised support that Saddam gets from the general population in Iraq, many Iraqis would be content to live their lives, get their paychecks, and raise their families without the stress caused on their country by their leader's military aspirations. Saddam, however, won't let go of his dream. In the *Babylon International Festival* brochure, Saddam states:

Old policies have always ignored the status of Babylon when they created psychological and scientific barriers between Iraqis and their leaders in ancient times. No one has ever mentioned the achievements of "Hammurabi," the founder of the first organized sets of law in human history. Or "Nebuchadnezzar," the national hero who was able to defeat the enemies of the nation on the land of "Kennan" ["Canaan"] and to take them as prisoner of war to Babylon. What we need now is an increased awareness in this regard.

There are several prophecies in the Bible that speak of the complete destruction of Babylon. Isaiah speaks about Babylon's doom that is coming in "the day of the Lord" (Isa. 13:6,9), that eschatological time when God will take over the affairs of planet earth in a very open and obvious way and "settle accounts."

Isaiah indicates that he is not talking about a past razing of Babylon through the invasion of one of Babylon's ancient enemies, but rather about a time of future judgment when the heavens will shake and God will punish the world for its sins (Isa. 13:10–13). The devastation upon Babylon will be so thorough that Babylon will become desolate like Sodom and Gomorrah and will no more be inhabited or dwelt in through all generations (Isa. 13:19–20; cf. also Jer. 51:26,43). From the very moment that God destroyed Sodom and Gomorrah, they ceased to exist. No tour company today can boast that you will take photos of Sodom and Gomorrah.

Two things are significant about these prophecies. First, Babylon has been inhabited consistently up to the present time. The Persians took Babylon quietly and by surprise. No great battles were fought that would have destroyed the city of Babylon and the nation. Daniel continued to serve God there under Darius, the Persian king, when Daniel was well advanced in years, perhaps eighty years of age according to the estimate of some (Dan. 6:1–2). Peter closes his first letter and states: "The church that is at Babylon, elected together with you, saluteth you" (1 Pet. 5:13).

Some take this as a cryptic reference to Rome, but there is no proof that Peter was ever in Rome, and many reasons for saying that he was never in Rome. Literal Babylon had a substantial Jewish community in the first century A.D. No, this final destruction of Babylon has not yet occurred. It is future.

The second thing that is significant is that neither America nor Great Britain is mentioned in connection with the final fall of Babylon. We are told that an alliance of nations will come against Babylon from the north and that this will occur when Israel is restored and seeks the Lord (Jer. 50:1–5).

What do we make of the absence of America in this final scenario? Some have suggested that America will cease to exist, and that this absence is proof of that. The Rapture will remove so many millions of Americans that American society will simply collapse. Others have offered the suggestion that America has been, at this point, absorbed by the European Union. Some have even suggested that the biblical picture of the demise of Babylon is really a biblical description of the demise of America.

While such questions are beyond the scope of this book, current events in the Middle East are developing at an amazing rate. The strong parallels between the news and Bible prophecy is an indicator of the lateness of the hour. "The might is far spent," we read in Romans 13:12, "the day is at hand: let us therefore cast off the works of darkness, and let us put on the armour of light."

Greece, Assyria, Syria, and Egypt

Much of Daniel 11 was fulfilled in the past. Though yet future when penned by Daniel, it shows the amazing accuracy of Daniel's prophecies and can be verified by examining history.

Daniel 11 opens by describing the wars and intrigues that involved the successors of Alexander the Great. When Alexander the Great died, his kingdom was divided be-

tween Cassander, Lysimmachus, Ptolemy, and Seleucus
I. Ptolemy received the area of Egypt, and Seleucus ruled
from what is now Syria. Before we examine the future
prophetic references, let's look at how accurately portions
of this ancient prophecy have already been fulfilled. This
will help us to see the certainty of Bible prophecy.

Verses 3–4 state: "And a mighty king shall stand up,
that shall rule with great dominion and do according to
his will, and do according to his will. And when he shall
stand up, his kingdom shall be broken, and shall be divided toward the four winds of heaven. . . ." The "mighty
king" is Alexander the Great who was one of the greatest
military leaders of all history.

Verse 6 explains that the king of the south (Egypt)
will come to the king of the north (Syria) and make an
"agreement." This refers to the attempt to unite Syria and
Egypt by a marriage alliance involving the Egyptian princess Berenice (daughter of Ptolemy II) and Antiochus
Theos (the Seleucid king of the north), but Berenice was
murdered.

Verse 7 explains subsequent events: "But out of a
branch of her roots," referring to Berenice's brother Ptolemy Euergetes, "shall one stand up in his estate, which
shall come with an army, and shall enter into the fortress
of the king of the north, and shall deal against them, and
shall prevail." Ptolemy avenged Berenice's death by conquering Syria. The inevitable result of this was continu-
ing conflict. Seleucus II waged war against Ptolemey
Philopator of Egypt (vs. 10).

Verse 17 states: "He shall also set his face to enter
with the strength of his whole kingdom, and upright ones
with him; thus shall he do: and he shall give him the
daughter of women, corrupting her: but she shall not

stand on his side, neither be for him." From 198 to 195 B.C. Antiochus attempted to control Egypt. A treaty was arranged between Antiochus and Ptolemy Epiphanes in which the former's daughter, Cleopatra—a "daughter of women," words applied to her since she was still so young as to be under the control of her mother—was espoused to Ptolemy. However, this treaty failed and Antiochus contented himself with conquering some islands along the Coast of Asia Minor (vs. 18).

Verse 20 describes Seleucus Philopator (187–170 B.C.): "Then shall stand up in his estate a raiser of taxes in the glory of the kingdom: but within few days he shall be destroyed, neither in anger, nor in battle." He was hated by the Jews because of his policy of taxation. He died "neither in anger, nor in battle," a reference to his death by poisoning.

Verses 21–35 provide a detailed picture of the role of the cruel Seleucid ruler, Antiochus Epiphanes, the last of the Seleucid rulers (175–163 B.C.), a type of the Antichrist, who brought extreme persecution and hardship on the Jewish people. To this we shall look in more detail.

The Present Alignment of These Nations and the Future

The prophetic Scriptures reveal that the kingdoms of the ancient world are very much alive in the end times and, significantly, they are very much alive today.

It is sometimes asserted that the four kingdoms mentioned in Daniel 2—Babylon, Medo-Persia, Greece, and Rome—are successively destroyed, but a study of the relevant scriptures reveals something entirely different. They are not destroyed successively in the past, but together at the time of the establishment of the Millennium Kingdom: "Then was the iron, the clay [Rome/Europe], the brass [Greece], the silver [Medo-Persia], and the gold [Babylon], *BROKEN TO PIECES TO-GETHER, and became like the chaff of the summer thresh-ing floors*" (Dan. 2:35). At our Pre-Trib Research Group meeting a few years ago I heard Philip Goodman, who had presented a paper dealing with Assyria in the future, make the point that when the great stone destroys the kingdom of the world, it is only at that time that Baby-lon, Persia, Greece, and Rome are destroyed once and for all.

While Daniel 11 describes the historical intrigues be-tween the Seleucid and Ptolemaic dynasties, the passage also propels us into the future. The Antichrist, who has been presented under the figure of the king of the North (Antiochus Epiphanes) is no longer identified with the king of the North.

In Daniel 11:40–41 we read: "And *at the time of the end* shall the king of the south push at *him*: and the king of the north shall come against *him* [a reference neither to the king of the north nor the king of the south, but a third figure, the Antichrist] like a whirlwind, with chari-ots, and with horsemen, and with many ships; and he shall enter into the countries, and shall overflow and pass over. *He* shall enter also into the glorious land. . . ." Here the kings of the north and south fight in the wars of the Antichrist.

A Middle Eastern Antichrist?

There can be no question but that the fourth empire of Daniel 2—the Roman—has a key role to play in end-time events. It is on the earth at the time of the establishment of the Millennial Kingdom (Dan. 2:44). It is important to remember, however, that when we speak of the Roman Empire and the people of that empire, that we are not simply speaking about people from the Italian Peninsula. The apostle Paul was a Roman, but he was not an Italian. The ancient Roman Empire included Western Europe—Britain and Spain—as well as the easternmost reaches of the empire—Egypt and Mesopotamia (Acts 22:3,25–29)—areas presented in the opening verses of Daniel 11, as discussed above. When we speak about the Revived Roman Empire of the future we are not warranted in limiting its scope to Western Europe.

Many prophetic scholars maintain that the Antichrist will be of Roman derivation. Some have argued against this, however, on the basis that, according to Daniel 9, the Jewish people accept the Antichrist as their Messiah. Since they would not accept a non-Jew as their Messiah, the Antichrist cannot be non-Jew. However, Daniel 9 does not say that the Jewish people will accept the Antichrist as their Messiah. It simply indicates that the Antichrist will confirm a covenant with them.

Among other things, this means that while the Antichrist may very well be Roman it does not necessitate that he will be European. To be Roman means that he will be from the Roman Empire. In the third century A.D. two Roman emperors—Elegabalus and his cousin Severus Alexander—were from the Middle East (Syria and Phoenicia).[71]

Chapter Ten

Objections To and Comments About Islam and Terrorism

1. *You don't read Arabic, so how can you pass judgment on a religion whose basic writings are in Arabic?*

There is no reason to believe that a good English translation of the Islamic writings does not reflect the true meaning of these documents. Converted Muslims who were raised reading and speaking Arabic testify that English translations adequately convey the spirit of Islam. Reading the Koran in Arabic does not lead one to conclude that Islam is essentially a peaceful religion. Obviously, many who read it in Arabic understand it as a mandate for war.

2. *There are many peace-loving Muslims who are good, moral people.*

This is absolutely true. Many Muslims have high moral

standards of honesty, integrity, and morality. Muhammad taught a religion that was far superior to the polytheistic religions of pre-Islamic Saudi Arabia. But while there are peaceful Muslims, that does not make Islam a peaceful religion. A Muslim who is peaceful is peaceful in spite of his or her religion. Similarly, while there have been, and are, Christians who wrongly advocate the use of violence, they are of this persuasion in spite of Christianity, not because of it.

3. You are promoting hatred of Muslims.
We are no more promoting hatred of Muslims than a book against pedophilia is promoting hatred of men. It is unfortunate that some men are pedophiles, but all men are not. Should we not expose the danger of pedophilia because it might adversely cast a shadow on all men?

4. Osama bin Laden was a civil engineer and was not trained in Islamic theology. His terrorist activities arise out of an ignorance of what Islam really teaches.
Sheikh Omar Abdel Rahman, presently serving a sentence in the U.S. for conspiring to destroy the World Trade Center in New York City, along with bridges and tunnels in 1993, holds a doctorate from Cairo's prestigious al-Azhar University, the world's oldest center for Muslim education. He is an Islamic cleric of the highest standing, even admired by bin Laden. This man is an Islamic religious leader who knows Islam. But he is also a murderous terrorist.

5. What right do you have to condemn someone else's religion?

We don't condemn anyone's religion. If we let Islam
speak for itself by looking at its Prophet, people, politics, and power we can learn much about Islam.

6. You Christians in America want freedom of religion for all religious groups except Islam. That is not fair.

We certainly support freedom of religion, even for
Muslims. However, in every country where Islam is
the rule of the land there is no religious freedom—
even though Muslims claim there is. Moreover, Islam
is more than a religion. It wants to establish a kingdom on earth and seeks to conquer the world for Allah. Those who won't submit are in grave peril. This
is not freedom of religion. This book, and others like
it, are not, therefore, trying to abolish freedom of religion but rather to maintain it.

7. You Christians have had your own holy wars— the Crusades, the Inquisition, and others. Why don't you look at your own history before maligning the history of Islam?

No rational individual can make a valid case for saying that the Crusades and other so-called "Christian
holy wars" were fought by the obedient followers of
Jesus Christ. It is impossible to find in the life of Jesus
either the precedent or approval of taking political
hostages or assassination or any other such barbaric
acts. Pope Urban II called the first Crusade into existence at the Council of Clermont (1095) and promised forgiveness of sins to Crusaders who died in battle. This is completely without biblical warrant. No
intelligent spokesman for the Christian faith would

try to justify such actions with an appeal to the New Testament.

8. When Timothy McVeigh murdered all of those people in Oklahoma City, no one blamed Christianity. Why do you blame Islam for the events of September 11?

Timothy McVeigh did not blow up the Federal Building because he was following the Bible. There is much evidence that he didn't even believe the Bible. On the other hand, the terrorists of September 11 left documents demonstrating that they were acting out of obedience to Islam.

9. The violence you find in the Koran comes from taking the Koran too literally.

Your objection indicts the Koran. If it can't be taken literally, then how do we know what it means? I can take the Christian Scriptures literally without misrepresenting Christianity. Why is there this problem that is uniquely associated with the Koran?

10. The Koran contains statements showing that there is to be no compulsion in religion and that Islam is a religion of peace.

Muhammad initially tried to win the favor of the Jews and Christians by seeking to persuade them that he was one of the Lord's true prophets. When they did not accept his claims, however, his attitude toward them changed radically. Furthermore, when Muhammad saw that his followers were few in number, he concluded that Allah had sent him only to warn and admonish. As his army grew in number and strength, however, he took a different approach.

Dialoguing With and Witnessing to Muslims

1. Muslims claim that the Bible has numerous errors and contradictions whereas the Koran has none.

If this is true, then why do Muslims quote from the Bible to prove that their religious views are correct? Why do they claim that the Bible really endorses Islam? Furthermore, Surah 10:94 actually recognizes that the Bible is authoritative. Is Surah 10:94 therefore in error?

There are passages in the Bible that seem to be contradictory, as in parallel accounts of the same events that give different numbers. All such seeming contradictions can be resolved in one or more of the following ways:

1. They are produced by a mistranslation;
2. They are due to a lack of knowledge of the customs and times the passage describes, and will be cleared up when more information is forthcoming, as has happened with so many other seeming contradictions that have now been carefully explained.
3. They are only apparent.
4. They are found in a corrupt manuscript. As I show in another section of this book, some of the "contradictions" in the genealogies are found in the modern translations using a corrupted text.

We should also point out that despite the claims of Muslims, the Koran also has "problem passages"—historical errors, contradictions, wrong names, and anachronisms—that Muslim apologists have to "explain." Various explanations are offered, some convincing, some not so convincing. The point is, the Koran has its problem passages, but in many Islamic nations no one dare mention them for fear of being punished.

2. *Muslims claim that the Bible also has its brutal and bloody passages. As proof of this they will point to Joshua, his battles, and the conquest of the Land of Canaan.*

The Divine command for the destruction of some of the cities of Canaan was for a specific people, a specific time and place, and for a specific purpose. Nowhere in the Old Testament, or in the New Testament, are we ever told that this is to be the normative practice for Christians for all time.

3. *Muslims claim that the Bible has been corrupted and altered to give favor to Jews and Christians. Some even claim that the name of Muhammad has been deliberately dropped from the Bible.*

As I indicated in an earlier chapter of this book, the burden of proof rests on Muslims who make this claim. It is up to them to prove their argument by coming up with very ancient manuscripts that show there was an earlier "Bible" that is different from the Bible of today. They haven't been able to do this because there is no "original Bible" that contradicts our present Bible.

Regarding the claim that Muhammad's name has been deliberately dropped from the Bible, this is like saying that the name of George Washington was deliberately dropped from Isaiah. Muhammad was born in A.D. 570. Why should we even expect his name to be in the Bible when the Bible was completed centuries before Muhammad was born?

4. **Muslims identify with Palestinians and are angry because America is considered an ally of Israel. Muslims support the formation of a Palestinian state.**

   This is a hotly-contested and emotional issue. Maps in Muslim schools in America and the Middle East omit "Israel" from the map as though it doesn't exist. While there is absolutely no basis for the Palestinian claim to this territory, it is best to avoid getting into a political issue. There are more important things to talk about.

5. **Many Muslims believe that Americans are corrupt, and that TV and Hollywood are destroying the moral fabric of America, as well as that of the entire world. Muslims also cite the high crime and divorce rates in America.**

   This is something that we can agree on. Let them know that you too are concerned and do not approve of the lifestyles of many Americans. Your honesty in this will help show that you do not "whitewash" the evils of contemporary American society.

6. **Muslims believe that many Americans are racists and that because many Muslims speak a different language, have a different skin color, and sometimes have a different style of dress, they are looked down on.**

   Unfortunately some Americans are racist. This is wrong. After September 11, Hindus and Sikhs were targeted by some Americans as being "Muslim." Their property, homes, stores, and automobiles were "torched." This is wrong, and especially tragic since Hindus and Sikhs have widely different beliefs than Muslims and are not to be identified with them.

Chapter Eleven

Has God Really Preserved His Word?

It is becoming increasingly obvious to the unbiased that the Bible has endured an unbelievable number of attacks from liberal critics, historians, scientists, cultists, and leaders of other religions. I use the word "endured" deliberately. Though the assaults keep coming, the Bible always manages to vindicate itself. Christian apologists (those who defend the Christian faith against the attacks of skeptics) continually show from archaeology, history, science, and other disciplines that what is stated in the Bible is indeed correct.

No doubt, no one is persuaded to become a Christian by proofs and argumentation. Ultimate conviction comes from the Holy Spirit who draws sinners to the Savior (John 6:44) and reveals how precious indeed is God's truth (1 Cor. 2:14-15). Yet, our part is still an important one. First Peter 3:15 states: ". . . be ready always to give an answer [apologian] to every man that asketh you a reason of the hope that is in you with meekness and fear."

In this chapter I will give "an answer" as to why Christians believe that the Bible is true and why we believe that not only was it true when it was originally given, but that God has preserved His Word and that we can demonstrate that fact.

This chapter will deal with two passages in the Bible that have been used by liberals, Muslims, and non-believers to show that the Bible contradicts itself, or is just plain wrong. In dealing with these two passages, we can develop an approach that will help us to understand some of the other passages that are often used against the Christian faith because they are allegedly in error.

Matthew's Genealogy

Several months ago a listener in Great Britain wrote that her daughter's professor at Cambridge University said that there were several errors in Matthew's genealogy. Since that time I have noticed that Muslims have also used some of the same arguments from this same passage. Before addressing the alleged errors, five important observations need to be made about Matthew's genealogy.

1. Matthew was writing in the style and manner of his day. It is faulty methodology to criticize Matthew by applying twenty-first–century historiographical criteria to a first-century document. Would the professor at Cambridge give Matthew a failing grade because he did not use footnotes and a selected bibliography?
2. Matthew is writing a *genealogy,* not a *chronology.* Matthew is not particularly interested in enabling his readers to compute the time span from the past to his

present. His interest is to show Jesus' pedigree. Since Matthew was writing to a Jewish audience, the apologetic value of his Gospel does not depend on giving an exact chronology, but it does depend on tracing the messianic line to Jesus.

3. Matthew is not always interested in presenting immediate descendants. "Son of" does not mean "immediate descendant of." This can be seen from Matthew 1:1: "The book of the generation of Jesus Christ, *the son of* David, *the son of* Abraham." While Jesus Christ is a descendant of David, He certainly is not the immediate descendant of David.

4. Matthew's theological focus can be seen in the fact that he includes women in his genealogy—a marked departure from standard practice in the ancient world. Actually, Matthew includes five women, some of whom had been involved in scandalous behavior: Tamar, the Canaanite woman who posed as a prostitute to seduce Judah (Gen. 38:13-30); Rachab, a Gentile and a prostitute; Ruth, a Moabite woman, a fact that made her offspring forbidden to enter the assembly of the Lord for ten generations (Deut. 23:3); Bathsheba, who committed adultery with David (2 Sam. 11); and Mary, a woman who drew the suspicion of her contemporaries because they thought she was pregnant outside of wedlock.

5. Matthew is obviously selective regarding the individuals whom he includes in his genealogy. Ishmael's name, for example, is not included because Matthew is presenting the messianic line.

After having stated these important principles for dealing with biblical genealogies, let's look at the particular "errors" that are alleged and see if they are, in fact, real errors or only imagined ones.

First alleged error: Rahab is listed as the mother of Boaz, but lived hundreds of years before Boaz was born.

Matthew 1:5 says that Boaz was "of Rachab." There is no error here because Mathew does not say that Rahab was "the mother of Boaz" or that she "gave birth to Boaz." He simply acknowledges that Boaz was a descendant of Rahab, which is factually true.

Second alleged error: Matthew seems to confuse Asaph the psalmist with King Asa.

Matthew does not confuse Asaph with King Asa in the traditional text of the New Testament, the *Textus Receptus* (TR). The confusion is created by the Nestle's Universal (NU) Text which erroneously reads "Asaph" instead of "Asa." The King James-traditional text reading of Matthew 1:7–8 agrees exactly with 1 Chronicles 3:10: "And Solomon's son was Rehoboam, Abia his son, Asa his son, Jehosphaphat his son."

Third alleged error: Matthew confuses the prophet Amos with King Amon.

The answer to this is the same as the answer above. The problem is not with Matthew, but with the NU Text which incorrectly reads "Amos." "Amon," which is the TR reading of Matthew 1:10 is correct.

Fourth alleged error: Josiah was the father of Jehoiakim, not Jeconiah.

In 1 Chronicles 3:14–16 we are told that Josiah was the father of Jehoiakim whose son was Jeconiah. So it is evident that Matthew skips a generation between Josiah and Jeconiah. In view of the other skips Matthew makes, and in view of Matthew's principles and purposes for his genealogy, this skip is not surprising.

Note that Matthew groups the individuals in his genealogy in three groups. Matthew 1:17 states: "So all the generations from Abraham to David are fourteen generations; and from David until the carrying away into Babylon are fourteen generations; and from the carrying away into Babylon unto Christ are fourteen generations."

Also note that Matthew counts Jeconiah twice and uses him to represent both the last generation before the Babylonian captivity and the first generation after. Since individuals are skipped, Matthew was deliberately seeking to create three groups, with fourteen names in each of the groups. Why?

Various reasons could be given. It could be that both the numbers "three" and "fourteen" are significant numbers from the standpoint of Bible numerics. Both "three" and "seven" are numbers associated with wholeness and completion and, "fourteen," being a multiple of "seven" might have given it a special appeal to Matthew. In this way Matthew was showing that Jesus Christ was perfectly qualified for His messianic role.

Or, Matthew may have created this scheme to assist those who were going to commit this genealogy to memory. Such would make it easier for first-century witnesses to share their faith in Christ with a Jewish audience.

Fifth alleged error: In Matthew 1:12 Matthew says Salathiel [Shealtiel] was the father of Zerubbabel, but 1 Chronicles 3:19 in the Masoretic Text says Pediah is the father of Zerubbabel.

On at least two occasions the Old Testament says that Zerubbabel was the son of Shealtiel. This can be verified from Haggai 1:1 and Nehemiah 12:1. So what Matthew writes is consistent with early Scripture. But how do we explain 1 Chronicles 3:19 where we are told that Zerubbabel was the son of Pediah?

First Chronicles 3:17–18 relates that Shealtiel and Pediah were brothers. It may be that though Pediah was the biological father of Zerubbabel, Shealtiel adopted Zerubbabel, his nephew, and was, for all intents and purposes, his father. In this case, "father" is being used to mean something other than "male parent," which is a manner of speech that we sometimes find in the Bible. That Jesus Christ is called "the Son of David" does not mean that David was His biological father.

"Twenty-two" or "Forty-two"

Enemies of the Bible seek to point to parallel passages that give conflicting data as proof that the Bible is less than the Word of God.

In 2 Kings 8:26 the King James Version of the Bible states that Ahaziah was twenty-two years old when he became king in Jerusalem. The parallel passage in 2 Chronicles 22:2, however, states that Ahaziah was forty-two years of age at the time he became king in Jerusalem. How could Ahaziah be twenty-two years of age when he became king, and also forty-two years of age when he became king?

There can be no reasonable doubt that these two passages are speaking about the same individual. Not only is Ahaziah specifically named, but in both passages we are told that Ahaziah's mother was Athaliah, the daughter of Omri.

If Ahaziah were forty-two years of age at the time of his accession to the throne, he would have been two years older than his father, Jehoram. Ahaziah's father, Jehoram was thirty-two years old when he became king and co-regent with Jehoshaphat. He ruled for eight years. If you add eight years to thirty-two years, you come out with an age of forty years (2 Kings 8:16–17). It is hard to see how a man could be two years older than his father.

Many scholars, even conservative ones, would dismiss this by simply saying that it is a "scribal error," or "an error in the transmission of the text." They would say that there was an error made by a copyist, or scribe who, because of tired eyes, poor lighting, or for some other reason, copied "forty-two" instead of "twenty-two." They would point out that this is not an error beyond being rectified or beyond being discerned because a little calculation would show that "twenty-two" is the correct age for Ahaziah and not "forty-two."

It would be easy to dismiss this as a scribal error, but what about God's promise to preserve His Word? In Psalm 12:6–7 we read: "The words of the LORD are pure words: as silver tried in a furnace of earth, purified seven times. Thou shalt keep them, O LORD, thou shalt preserve them from this generation for ever."

It is possible that Ahaziah was adopted. Theoretically, this would allow him to be older than his so-called "father." However, there is no indication of this anywhere in the Bible. It is best to hold that Ahaziah was twenty-two years of age when he became King of Israel.

But if that is true, then how are we to understand the statement in 2 Chronicles 22:2 that he was forty-two at the time of his accession to the throne?

Dr. Floyd Nolen Jones, in his detailed chronological

study, *Chronology of the Old Testament: A Return to Basics,* has done a complete and exhaustive study of this issue and related issues that have plagued Christian apologists and have seemed to defy reconciliation and satisfactory explanation.

Dr. Jones has a degree in mathematics and is also seminary trained. In addition to his book on Bible chronology he has written an excellent book entitled *Which Version Is the Bible?* He is a careful scholar who demonstrates from Scripture, science, and history that Ussher's chronology is correct. In his *Chronology of the Old Testament,* Dr. Jones makes a couple of important observations that shed much light on the question that we are addressing.

He points out that in both passages the word "was" is in italics, meaning that it was supplied by the King James translators to make the English reading smoother, but that it is not in the Masoretic Text. The Hebrew literally reads that Ahaziah was "a son of forty-two years." Second Chronicles 22:2 does not say that Ahaziah was forty-two years old when he became king, but rather that when he became king he was "a son of forty-two years."

What is represented by the forty-two years? The forty-two years is a reference to the number of years that had transpired since the beginning of the dynasty of Omri, of which Ahaziah was a member through Athaliah. In fact, 2 Chronicles 22:2 actually states that Ahaziah's mother was "Athaliah the daughter of Omri."

We can emphatically state, therefore, that in the Masoretic Text there is no contradiction. The Hebrew of the Masoretic Text does not say that Ahaziah was forty-two years old when he became king, but rather, that he became king in the forty-second year of the dynasty of Omri.

This was the method of counting time used by the human author of 2 Chronicles. There is a statement concerning Baasha which has also prompted some to say that there is a so-called "copyist's error" in the text.

It is seen when comparing 1 Kings 16:8 and 2 Chronicles 16:1. How can Baasha be said to come up against Asa in the thirty-sixth year of Asa's reign when another scripture declares that Baasha died in the twenty-sixth year of Asa's reign?

The solution is to realize tht Chronicles is referencing the thirty-six years *from the division of the monarchy and the beginning of the Judaic dynasty of Asa.* "Hence," writes Jones, "the Hebrew phrase which includes the 'reign' of Asa in 2 Chronicles 16:1 references the kingdom over which Asa had dominion and is to be understood in the sense of 'the kingdom of Asa' (Judah) as distinguished from the northern kingdom, *not* the number of years he had occupied the throne in actual reign" (p. 144).

Some of the modern translations of the traditional text seek to faithfully translate the text of 2 Chronicles 22:2, and in doing so the problem disappears. For exmple, both the *King James II* translation and also the *Modern King James* translation render 2 Chronicles 22:2 in this way: "Ahaziah's dynasty was forty-two years old when he began to reign." The passage is not speaking about Ahaziah's age when he became king. It is speaking about the age of the dynasty of which Ahaziah was a part.

"The Mysterious Numbers of the Hebrew Kings"

One of the most difficult challenges to the doctrine of the Divine inspiration of the Scriptures and their preservation has been in the area of harmonizing the lengths of the reigns of the kings given in different books of the Old Testament.

Of particularly perplexing difficulty is harmonizing the reigns for the rulers of Israel and Judah as found in Kings and Chronicles. When a king of one nation ascended the throne, a synchronism was given with a ruler of the other nation who becomes a reference point. For example, regarding Jehoahaz, king of Israel, 2 King 13:1 states: "In the three and twentieth year of Joash the son of Ahaziah king of Judah Jehoahaz the son of Jehu began to rein over Israel in Samaria." The same pattern is followed in 2 Kings 14:1,2 where we are told of Amaziah of Judah that "in the second year of Joash son of Jehoahaz king of Israel reigned Amaziah the son of Joash king of Judah." Sometimes the synchronization is stated in terms of the number of years the ruler of one nation lived after the death of the ruler of the other nation: "And Amaziah the son of Joash king of Judah lived after the death of Jehoash son of Jehoahaz king of Israel fifteen years" (2 Kings 14:17).

The problem is that the precise data given in the biblical text often becomes the source of much debate since the numbers appear to be in contradiction with each other. For centuries it has been impossible to explain or reconcile the difficulties, or to establish a convincing harmony with the chronology of ancient history. In other words the synchronisms don't seem to synchronize.

In two scholarly works, *A Chronology of the Hebrew Kings* (1977) and *The Mysterious Numbers of the Hebrew King* (1983), Dr. Edwin R. Thiele has solved virtually every synchronistic problem by explaining the methodology used by the ancient chroniclers.

He has shown, among other things, that an item of

vital importance was the method of counting the first year of a ruler's reign. Two different methods were employed by the biblical historians of the northern and southern kingdoms, and sometimes the method changed within the same kingdom. Was the first year of a king's reign counted as year one, or was his second year counted as year one? In accession-year reckoning, year one began with the first full year. In nonaccession-year dating, the first year was considered year one.

Accession-year reckoning:
(accession year)   (year one)   (year two)

Nonaccession-year reckoning:
(year one)   (year two)   (year three)

Kings in a nation using accession-year reckoning will always be one year behind in total number of years reigned than kings in a nation using nonaccession-year dating. The nation that uses the latter will always have more years recorded for the same period of time than a nation using the former system. Not knowing the system used will lead some to conclude that there is an error in the text when, in fact, there is none.

Moreover, since under a nonaccession-year system the last year of a previous king was reckoned as the first year of his successor, that year is counted twice, meaning that in a nonaccession system a reign reckoned in this manner was one year higher than absolute time. When there are a series of kings in a nation using nonaccession dating, the total number keeps on increasing by one year over absolute time by one year for every king. Hence, when seeking to relate the reign of a king to absolute time, one year must be deducted from each reign.

Thiele has carefully studied the variations between the Hebrew Masoretic Text (MT) and the Septuagint (LXX) and has concluded that the variations are the result of deliberate editorial changes made by the translators of the LXX with the object of removing the "contradictions." However, because the translators of the LXX were ignorant of the method of time reckoning used by the ancients, rather than improving the text, the translators produced a Greek translation with many chronological errors. Thiele writes, "In no instance is a Greek variation an improvement over the Hebrew."[72]

Thiele has thoroughly investigated and explained various other chronological methodologies employed by the ancient Hebrew historians and has validated both the Hebrew Masoretic Text as well as the minute accuracy of the Old Testament Scriptures.

Much more could be said about this, but additional detail would take us far beyond the scope of this brief work and will be detailed in a future book on which I am currently working. Suffice it to say, the "errors" that are supposed to be in the text of Scripture are really not errors.

End Notes

1. "The Islamic Agenda and its Blueprints," *http://answering-islam.org/Terrorism/ agenda.html,* 12/4/02, p. 1.

2. Robert A. Morey, *Winning the War Against Radical Islam* (Christian Scholars Press, 2002), p. 149.

3. Ibid., pp. 48–49.

4. Ibid., pp. 55–56.

5. John Ankerberg and John Weldon, *Fast Facts on Defending Your Faith* (Eugene, OR: Harvest House, 2002), p. 135.

6. *A Dictionary of Early Christian Beliefs,* ed. By David W. Bercot (Peabody, MA: Hendrickson Publishers, 1998), pp. 558–559.

7. Ergun Caner and Emir Caner, *Unveiling Islam* (Grand Rapids: Kregel, 2002), p. 118.

8. Gary Redman, "An Explanation of the Trinity for Muslims," *http://debate.org.uk/ topics/theo/trinity.htm,* 12/4/02, p. 4.

9. Ron Rhodes, *Reasoning from the Scriptures with Muslims* (Eugene, OR: Harvest House, 2002), p. 114.

10. Redman, p. 35.

11. Ibid., p. 18.

12. Robert A. Morey, *The Trinity: Evidence and Issues* (Grand Rapids: World Publishing, 1996), p. 436.

13. Karen Armstrong, *Islam* (New York: Modern Library, 2000), p. 17.

14. William Spencer, *Islamic Fundamentalism in the Modern World* (Brookfield, CT: The Millbrook Press, 1995), pp. 15–17.

15. William H. Banks, Jr., *The Black Muslims* (Philadelphia: Chelsea House Publishers, 1997), p. 9.

16. Ibid., pp. 10–11.

17. Ibid., pp. 11–13.

18. Jennifer Harper, "PBS Show to 'Counter' Perceptions of Islam," *www.washtimes.com/ national/20021213-91496698,* (12/14/02), pp. 1–2.

19. Anis Shorrosh, Watchman on the Wall interview with Larry Spargimino, aired Friday, Nov. 15, 2002.

20. Saleem Almahdy, "Islam and Egypt: Pyramids or Persecution." *Voice of the Martyrs* (12/02), p. 9.

21. *www.whitehouse.gov/infocus/ramadan/islam.html,* 11/8/02.

22. Harper, p. 2.

23. *WorldNetDaily.com/news/article.asp?ARTICLE_ID=29885,* 12/20/02, p. 3.

24. "The Islamic Agenda and its Blueprints."

25. Martin Kramer, "Islam Presents an Obstacle to Democracy." In *Islam: Opposing Viewpoints* (San Diego: Greenhaven Press, 2001), p. 40.

26. Deanna Othman, "Women fare well under Islam." *Dallas Morning News* (12/25/ 02).

27. Ibid.

28. Ibn Warraq, "Islam Supports Gender Inequality." In *Islam: Opposing Viewpoints*, pp. 86–87.

29. Gihan El Gindy, *Seeing Through the Veil* (Washington D.C: Transcultural Educational Center, n.d.).

30. Ibid.
31. Jean Sasson, *Princess: A True Story of Life Behind the Veil in Saudi Arabia* (New York: William Morrow, 1992), front flap.
32. Ibid., pp. 94–95.
33. Shorrosh, Ibid.
34. Sasson, pp. 216–217.
35. Ibid., p. 21.
36. Anis A. Shorrosh, *Islam Revealed—A Christian Arab's View of Islam* (Nashville: Thomas Nelson, 1988), pp. 49–66.
37. "Religion of 'Peace': More than 450 Muslim women killed in Pakistan during 2002 in name of 'honor,'" *www.jewishwrldreview.com/12/02 honor_killings.asp*, 12/14/02, pp. 1–2.
38. Ibn Warraq, pp. 87–88.
39. Quoted from M. Rafiqul-Haqq and P. Newton, "The Place of Women in Pure Islam," *http://debate.domini.org/newton/women.html*, 12/3/02, p. 25.
40. Ibn Warraq, p. 91.
41. Rafiqul-Haqq and Newton, p. 25.
42. Ibid., p. 11
43. Robert W. Tracinski, "Islamic Terrorism Poses a Threat to the United States." In *Islam: Opposing Viewpoints*, p. 109.
44. Rhodes, pp. 83–84.
45. Tom Masland, "Fatwas: To Kill or Not To Kill," *Newsweek* (12/19/02), p. 10.
46. Barbara Slavin, "Saudis dispute terror critics," *USA Today* (12/4/02), p. 1-A.
47. Daniel Pipes, "Islam Suppresses Freedom of Speech. In *Islam: Opposing Viewpoints*, pp. 58–60.
48. Robin Wright, "Islam Does Not Present an Obstacle to Democracy." In *Islam: Opposing Viewpoints*, p. 49.
49. Ibid., p. 51.
50. Pipes, pp. 61–62.
51. Ali A Marzui, "Claims that Islam Suppresses Freedom of Speech Are Hypocritical." In *Islam: Opposing Viewpoints*, p. 68.
52. Pipes, p. 57.
53. Haroon Siddiqui, "U.S. Policies Incite Islamic Terrorism." In *Islam: Opposing Viewpoints*, p. 147.
54. Ibid.
55. Oubai Shahbandar, "Why they hate me: An Arab student speaks out," *WorldNetDaily.com/news/article.asp?ARTICLE_ID=30101*, 12/20/02, p. 2.
56. Published by the King Fahd Complex for the Printing of the Holy Qur'an, Madina, K.S.A.
57. Caner and Caner, pp. 48–49.
58. Taken from Rhodes, p. 205.
59. Winfried Corduan, *Islam: A Christian Introduction* (Downers Grove, IL: Inter-Varsity Press, 1998), p. 29.
60. Some of this material is taken from "The Deadliest End-Times Gamble" which I co-authored with Dr. Bob Glaze and which appeared in the November 2002 *Prophetic Observer.*
61. Morey, *Winning the War*, p. 203.
62. *apnew.excite.com*, 10/11/02.

63. *WorldNetDaily.com,* 10/3/02, pp. 2–3.

64. John Leo, "Rage Is Not the Rage," *U.S. News & World Report,* 9/16/02, p. 10.

65. Charles Krathammer, "The Case for Profiling: Why random searches of airline travelers are a useless charade," *Time,* 3/18/02, p. 104.

66. Ibid.

67. *http://newsmax.com/archives/articles/2002/8/16/61426.shtml* (9/10/02), p. 1.

68. Nidal M. Ibrahim, "From the Editor's Desk—A Glimpse of the Future," *Arab-American Business: The Magazine for a Culture of Success,* 7/02, p. 6.

69. *http://newsmax.com,* 9/10/02, p. 2.

70. "What the Muslims in Britain Want," *Israel Today,* 10/02, p. 9.

71. Phillip Goodman, *The Assyrian Connection* (LaFayette, LA: Prescott Press, 1993), p. 46.

72. Edwin R. Thiele, *The Mysterious Numbers of the Hebrew Kings* (Grand Rapids: Academie Books, 1983), p. 210.